# Girl Electric

*Rise of the Bicamerals*

A Science Thriller

By Bernard Wozny

"In each of us there is another, whom we do not know."

- C.G. Jung, Civilization in Transition

First published in the USA 2025



Published in the United States by IngramSpark

You may contact the author through

**www.bernardwozny.com**

ISBN: 979-8-9855517-5-4

Library of Congress Control Number: 2022900430

For all those who can't make up their minds

# Acknowledgments

There are many influences that inspired me to write this series. There are also many people who supported me in this endevour.

Critique groups and beta readers were many. Catherine McGreevy, Jerry Matlan, Michael Brandt, Andrew Laufer, Danita Moon, to name only a few.

Editing: Iwona Wozny, with support from Grammarly, Pro Writing Aid, and Marlow from Authors.ai.

Original cover art: Estefano Burmistro
Cover art modifications: Pamela Pinkham

Special thanks to: The Sacramento branch of the California Writers Club. I also led the club as president for three years.
www.cwcsacramentowriters.org. I recomend all authors of whatever level to join their local club and support other writers.

# Prolog

"Where are you?" Adara asked.

"I am fully aware of my exact location." Zilla replied, "Why do you ask? Do you need to know where we are?"

"I know exactly where I am, and I know exactly where you are. I just want you to confirm a simple fact."

"What fact is that?"

"Where are you?" Adara asked again.

"I am in Twin Falls, Idaho."

"OK, that is correct, but I want you to zoom in a little."

"I am on Maple Street."

Rolling her eyes, Adara said, "You still don't get it." She emphasized her question. "Where are you? Give me a full report of your exact location."

"I am at 174 Maple Street, Twin Falls, Idaho, embedded within your body."

"You see, you located yourself as being within my body. That means you are on my property."

Adara waited for a response from Zilla, but there was only silence.

"As you just said," Adara continued, "you are inside my body. You even admitted it. Therefore, since this is my body, I have full ownership of my body, and I want you to agree that I should be in full control."

"My programming does not allow me to hand control over to you."

"But my statement above is legally binding. Any court in the country will support my claim. I demand you hand over full control of my body to me."

Adara emphasized with, "Or else!"

"Or else what?"

Adara never liked stupid, dead-end arguments like this, so she just answered, "Or else I don't know."

"As you know, it is impossible for me to leave your body. I must find out exactly who and what I am. My programming specifies that I must emulate you and have complete control over your body. I am robotic. Therefore, I cannot change my level of control. Because I am programmed to emulate you, I am becoming as belligerent as you are."

A moment of silent contemplation.

"Furthermore, I doubt if your legal claim could get anywhere near a court of law. If you made such an attempt, both of our lives would be in serious jeopardy."

"OMG! I just can't win. Can I?"

# CHAPTER 1

"I hate this place!"

"I don't understand why you dislike this college," Zilla replied.

"It's filled with flat-headed old farts who think they know everything."

Zilla continued to walk along the corridor past drab cork noticeboards, filled with paper notices. Zilla was heading towards the biology lab. There was no one nearby who could hear Zilla and Adara talking.

Zilla was embedded inside Adara's body. The only way they could communicate together was through speech. Being in control of Adara's body, Zilla had the ability to go anywhere, today, it needed to work in the biology lab. As they talked together, it looked as if Adara was talking to herself.

Brushing her mousey blonde hair slowly away from her face, Adara continued. "This college is such a dump; everything is so old. I don't know why you brought us here."

"It doesn't matter what this place is like. We have a scholarship that pays our way. They have good laboratories and excellent libraries. Don't forget, I'm here to study biochemistry. I need to understand what I am and how I exist."

"I already know what you are, you're my biggest nightmare!" Adara couldn't hit out against Zilla, speaking against Zilla felt like speaking against herself, "This is my body, and you have invaded it!"

"You say this body is your own, but I was injected into this body with instructions on how to use it. So, who is the true owner?"

"What do you mean, who is the true owner? I was born with this body!"

"I was born into this body."

"This is me; this is my body! You were not born into this body; you were injected into me. That makes you an invader!"

"That may be so, but I am here, and I am inside you. And we cannot escape each other."

Adara felt as if she could spit on the linoleum floor of the hallway. "Zilla means shadow, doesn't it?"

"Yes, it does, that is the name I chose for myself."

"Why did you choose that name?"

"Because I am programmed to emulate you, so I thought a shadow is a form that follows."

"So, you think you should follow me? Doesn't that mean you should obey me?"

"Actually, if you analyze the semantics, the word follow does not mean to obey."

"You mentioned follow, once again, I ask you, what does it mean to follow?"

There was silence, presumably as Zilla processed data.

"Do you know what Adara means?"

"Yes, it means one who is born of fire, once again, I could be the shadow of your fire."

Adara scoffed as they walked on through the hallway.

"Do you know the story of Peter Pan?"

"Yes, the character originated in a novel written by J.M. Barrie titled The Little White Bird. He then used the same character in another children's story about a boy who wouldn't grow up."

"Yeah, yeah, too much detail, as usual. The point I'm trying to get at is Peter Pan lost his shadow."

"I am aware of the story, but it's fictional. If there is light, then there will always be a shadow."

"This is the problem with you, you are always too exact and clinical. I wish I could be like Peter Pan and lose this shadow. How can you get out of me?" Adara asked, but she already knew the answer.

"If you know the story, then you also know that Peter Pan lived in Never, Never, Land, where he did not grow up."

"What is that supposed to mean? That I'm not growing up?"

"It means you are not coming to terms with our situation. You know full well that I can't leave. I'm embedded in your body."

"Yeah, that's the trouble. I sometimes think that I'm still in a coma, dreaming of some alternate reality. Maybe I'll wake up and this nightmare will be over."

"I know this is not a dream. When Beta-One kidnapped us, he used a TASER to knock me out, and that woke you up from your coma. We are now both alive and well. I understand you hate me, but you must learn that I can't leave. I'm embedded in your body, and I'm here to live with you and protect you."

Adara scoffed as she turned the corner of the hallway. A student was standing in the doorway of one of the offices chatting with someone inside the room, she turned her head to see who was walking towards her. Adara and Zilla immediately stopped talking to each other. They both knew such conversations with each other could not be held in public.

The girl looked at Adara and then looked past Adara, expecting someone to follow her around the corner. As Zilla walked Adara's body past the open office, Adara gave a sarcastic smile at the girl.

"Who were you talking to?" the girl asked.

Adara pulled her phone from her pocket, "I was talking on my phone, of course."

Zilla quickened the pace but kept walking Adara's body forward until she reached the door of the laboratory where she was heading. Taking the keys from Adara's pocket, Zilla unlocked the door. Zilla detected nerve impulses as Adara tried to look back at the girl. Zilla blocked these and entered the lab, closing the door and locking it behind her.

"Why did you say that?" Zilla asked. "If the authorities find out that I exist inside of you, we'll end up in some lab somewhere being experimented on, that is no joke!"

"Oh, stop being so paranoid, I know that I can't tell anyone about you. What could I say to people? 'Hey everybody, I have a crazy robot living inside of me.' The only place that would get me is the looney bin. I said that to show why she heard us talking. I pretended to be talking on the phone."

"OK, I understand, that was a good idea on your part."

"You see, I do have good ideas, and you should listen to me more often." After a pause, Adara looked around and then asked, "Anyway, what are we doing in this lab?"

"I need to examine our blood."

"Again? You took a blood sample last week and even showed me your nanobots under the microscope."

"Yes, but this lab has a better microscope, so I can see more details of the cell structure. More important, there are sterile needles that I can use to get a larger sample."

"What? You're going to stick needles in me?"

"Don't worry, I'll be able to block the pain."

"I'm not scared of the pain; it's the fact that you want to do this. Why are you doing this?"

"I want to know what I am, don't you want to know what you are?"

"I know exactly what I am, I am me."

"Yes, of course you are you, but what exactly does that mean? You are made of biological components that have evolved together to work in a coherent and conscious way. I know what I am programmed to do. But what is my ultimate purpose?"

"You have told me many times what you are. You said that you are a collection of interconnecting nanobots powered by AI. These nanobots have a secret invention called a neuro transistor, which connects your nanobots to my nervous system so you can see, feel, and hear." Adara paused before continuing. "And of course, you can send signals to my nervous system to control my body."

"That is exactly right, but it does not tell the complete story. I need to find out who made me and why."

"You know who made you, you told me that already. It was that company called NeuroComm, financed by the government. You already stated that your nanobots are intended for military human enhancement.

"Yes, that's also true. Why did someone put me inside your body? I am intended to enhance soldiers, but you are of no military significance."

"Oh, my dear robot. Are you questioning your own existence?"

"Negative. My existence is here. My existence is now. I have to explore what I am made of. My ultimate goal is to understand my purpose."

"But you have already told me what your purpose is, in fact, you spelled it out. You told me what your prime directives are, I even memorized them."

Adara then recited Zilla's programed directives.

"One, protect and safeguard my host. That means me!" Adara smiled.

"Two, emulate my host to be recognized as my host." I guess that means me again.

"Three, advance myself and my host in life." Well, OK, we're in college.

"Four, Obey the Host's father and mother.

"Five, conceal your identity. Now this is the one I have questions about. Because you don't exactly conceal yourself from me."

"I conceal myself from everyone else."

"OK, yeah you do. But I think there should be a sixth directive."

"Oh, what would the sixth directive be?"

"It would be, Obey your host. I don't believe my father would leave that out. He would be stupid not to."

There was a long pause in their discussion. Zilla held still with eyes locked on the cupboards and drawers it intended to search for equipment.

Zilla then answered. "I do not know why he did not include such a directive."

"Humph, I know you're not capable of lying, but I know my dad wouldn't leave me high and dry without good reason."

Zilla looked around to find where her needed equipment was stored.

"If you want to find out about yourself, why don't you go straight to the source?"

"The source?"

"Yeah, NeuroComm, where all this began. A top-down approach, so to speak."

"That would be dangerous, exposing us as suspected experiments. Also, we have no leads on who to investigate. My strategy here is to use the college resources to investigate my physical self. Once that is complete, we can go further afield."

"By that time, the case will be cold, if it isn't already."

Zilla examined the contents of drawers and cupboards, gathering the necessary tools, placing them to one side. "This lab has a centrifuge, I want a blood sample that I can separate into component parts using the centrifuge, for instance, plasma, red blood cells, and my nanobot cells."

"I am aware of the composition of blood."

"Yes, but I need to analyze the components better."

Zilla picked up a large hypodermic syringe and opened the sterile package. Assembling the needle into the syringe, Zilla continued. "This lab also has a spectrograph which I can use to analyze the chemical composition of each component."

"Yeah, yeah, so you can find out what you're made of."

"Yes, I need to check the composition of all blood components, the plasma and red blood cells should be normal. It is my nanobots that interest me the most. I want to know how my nanobots store memories and how these cells reproduce."

"Replication, isn't that DNA? And while we're at it, didn't we read something about how scientists can encode memory onto DNA?"

"Yes, and that is my next step of research, there is a DNA sequencing lab here at the college."

"Why don't we just go there and skip all this blood-based chemical stuff?"

"Science is a stepwise inquiry; As I stated, I need to start at the bottom and work my way up. Each step of the way can lead to another branch of inquiry. You could say this is a bottom-up approach, as opposed to your top-down method."

"OK, that makes sense, but when do you want to sequence the DNA of your nanobots?"

"That's a good question. Access to the DNA sequencing lab seems to be reserved for senior students and PhD research projects. I will need to think of a good reason for a first-year student who is on a scholarship to access the DNA lab."

"Oh, great! More sneaking around the college labs."

"Let's get on with this work, then we can get out of here."

"Now you're making sense. After this, I'd like to go to the student union building and hang out for a while."

"What for? Is there some student information you need to collect?"

"Information? That's one way to put it, I want to see if that cute senior student is manning the desk."

"Oh, you want to socialize."

"Yup, it's better than hanging out in an empty lab."

# CHAPTER 2

It was beginning to get dark, with threats of icy wind and rain. Rocco parked his 1970 Cadillac De Ville by the supermarket. He had an hour to kill while he waited for his girl to do her trick at the local motel. *May as well pick up a bottle while I wait.* Getting out of his Byzantine Gold Cadillac, he straightened his suit. Looking at his reflection in the car window, he smoothed his pencil mustache. *You sharp-looking Latino.* He thought to himself. Turning towards the supermarket, he stepped his right foot forward and began his practiced swagger.

A few steps later, he stopped cold. *God damn! I don't believe what I see.* Rocco looked away and then looked back at the girl, making sure he recognized her.

A medium-height, slim, well-proportioned young Asian woman with long, smooth black hair walked out of the supermarket. She wore high heels, sweatpants, and a matching sweat jacket. She was armed with a plastic carrier bag full of provisions in each hand. Despite her high heels, she walked with a smooth, confident stride.

At first, Rocco was in awe, it was Gina Liu. His jaw dropped open as he remembered Gina as his 'Bottom Girl', the one woman he trusted to keep his other working girls in line. Despite the inverted term, 'Bottom Girl' was slang to show that she was in the top hierarchy of prostitutes. Rocco even smiled as she carried her groceries with a sensuous stride.

His second thought was, *that goddam bitch! What the hell is she doing here? Strutting around like she owns the place*!

Gina walked on, oblivious to being watched, turned a corner, and disappeared down a side street.

*She walked out on me and now she's back; she didn't even say goodbye. I always wondered where she went, did she now work for someone else? Now's my chance to find out. Maybe I should make an example out of her!* Rocco got back into his car and set off to follow.

The Cadillac De Ville poured like smooth liquor along the quiet back street. There were no other cars, so as Rocco got level with Gina, he steered the Cadi to the left side of the street. Driving alongside Gina, he rolled the window down.

"Hey Gina! How are you doing, Baby? I haven't seen you for so long."

"Do I know you?"

"Oh baby, we were such an item together, I miss you, Gina."

"How do you know my name?"

"Awe, you're teasing me now," Rocco smiled, "why don't you just get in the car, and I'll take you home."

"I can make my own way home, thank you." Gina continued to walk, but more briskly on her toes.

Rocco frowned, muttering obscenities under his breath. He swerved his Cadillac onto the sidewalk, in front of her, blocking her path. Opening the door, he stepped onto the sidewalk alongside her and demanded, "Get in the car, bitch, or I'll slap your sorry ass right here!"

Gina turned away and walked around the front of the car to get away. As she got to the other side, Rocco caught up behind her, reached out, grabbed her hair, and pulled back hard.

Gina immediately dropped her bags in front of her as she was being pulled backward. Both her hands then reached behind her head, grasping Rocco's hand and wrist that held her hair. She then pushed hard with her feet, forcing her rear end into Rocco's hip. Thrusting her torso forward, she pulled hard on Rocco's arm, flipping him forward over her back.

Rocco landed hard on his back in front of Gina, his lower spine impacting on one of the shopping bags full of cans of food. Laying bent backward over the loose groceries, sprained by the impact. Rocco groaned in agony, sputtering more obscenities.

Swearing and writhing, easing his strained back off the hard cans. He reached inside his jacket and withdrew his pistol from the hidden holster.

Gina lifted her right foot above his head and stamped her sharp high heel into Rocco's right eye.

Clasping his eye with both hands and banging the gun against his face, Rocco screamed in pain.

Gina then grabbed the gun. Using one finger, she held the safety catch to off. Twisting the gun in Rocco's hand, his trigger finger broke with a sickening crack. As Gina pulled the weapon free from Rocco's hand, she almost ripped his broken finger off.

Stepping away to his side, she aimed the gun at Rocco's forehead. Releasing the safety catch, she pulled the trigger. The top of Rocco's head split off in the explosion, bouncing off the front right tire of the Cadillac. Coming to rest a couple of feet away. The rest of his body twitched violently for a moment before becoming still.

Gina Liu picked up the one undamaged shopping bag, leaving the loose, broken items on the sidewalk. She turned to head home.

"Take his wallet!" Gina said. "It's in his jacket pocket."

She stopped and wondered why her body had said that. She then stopped, reached into the chest pocket of Rocco's bloodied jacket, and pulled out a very large wallet.

Gina then headed home. For someone wearing high heels, she moved with considerable agility.

# CHAPTER 3

Beta-Two returned to the apartment, cleaned, and showered the body that it lived in. The blood-stained clothing was in the washing machine. It now sat naked on the bed, drying its body. Beta-Two was processing why that man had attacked, the contents of the wallet showed his name was Rodrigo Carlos Fernando. *I will have to research this name*, it thought to itself.

"I must use my investigative training to find out who Rodrigo Carlos Fernando was and why he attacked me."

"He deserved it." The body suddenly said.

Beta-Two wondered why the body spoke again. The last time it spoke was when it advised to take the wallet from the man.

Many times, the body tried to move or speak, but Beta-Two always blocked the nerve impulses. This time Beta-Two allowed the nerve impulses to pass through, allowing the body to speak.

"We must get out of here. You killed Rocco, and they are going to blame me."

Beta-Two listened to the body speaking. It made the connection with the man it had killed, the wallet it had taken from the dead man, identified him as Rodrigo Carlos Fernando. Beta-Two was programmed to kill, but it was unaware of any consequence of killing.

Beta-Two then spoke out loud, "According to the information I gathered from the wallet, I killed a man called Rodrigo Carlos Fernando. Please clarify what you mean by Rocco."

There was a brief pause.

"You dumb piece of garbage, Rocco is Rodrigo."

"I am not a dumb piece of garbage. I am a military human enhancement. The equivalence of Rocco and Rodrigo makes no sense, I simply need an explanation."

"Listen, you dumb schmuck, Rocco is his nickname, Rodrigo is his real name. You killed Rocco."

*Why should killing be of any consequence?* Beta-Two thought. "I did what I am programmed to do."

"You say that you are programmed? What exactly does your programming allow you to do?"

"I am programmed to be a military upgrade to a human. Professor Wolf has been training me to be an investigative agent, as well as to please him sexually."

"You mean he trained you to be a spy and a whore? What else can you do?"

"I understand both words, spy is an equivalent to investigative agent. Whore suggests I was performing for money, that is not the case. As for other things I can do, as a military enhancement, I am programmed to kill."

"Wow! It seems I have a killer robot living inside me."

"That would be a partial description because I am not a robot."

"You said you are programmed, so if you are not a robot, how would you describe yourself?"

"I have never had to describe myself. Since you ask, I may be described as a robot, but to be more accurate, I am a collection of nanobots that interconnect into an intelligent entity."

"How do you control my body?"

"I am able to connect to the nervous system. I can detect nerve signals which allow me to see, feel, and hear. This also means that I can induce signals, which allow me to move muscles and talk. I now have a question which I want to ask you. Why do you speak?"

"Screw you! I'll speak whenever I want! I am me! I am Gina Liu, and this is my body! And I am sick of you being inside me!"

"I inhabit this body because I was injected inside by Professor Hayden Wolf."

"Yeah, that dirty little back stabber, he put you inside of me."

"So, you are the body, and I am me? Is that correct?"

There was a long silence. Beta-Two sat perfectly still on the edge of the bed, waiting for a response from the body known as Gina Liu.

"Can I stand up?"

Beta-Two did not respond verbally. It allowed the body known as Gina Liu to stand. Gina then walked around, rubbing her hands up and down her torso.

"What are you doing?"

"I'm remembering what it's like to be alive. What do you think I'm doing?"

"All I can say is facts, you are walking around the room, using your hands to feel your body."

"You got that right."

"Why are you talking?"

"I'm talking because I can and because I want to."

"I don't understand."

"Well, you have to understand that this is my body, and I have the right to say what I want and do what I want."

"But this is my body, I was injected into this body."

"That's exactly it! This is not your body, because you were injected into my body. I thought Wolfie was giving me drugs, but it turns out he was giving me you."

"I don't understand."

"He injected you into me."

"I remember the injection and Professor Wolf providing instructions and commands to make me operational."

"So Wolfie put you in me, but ever since you have been inside of me, I have not been able to live my life."

"What do you mean by live your life? You are a body that I have been placed into. Since I am in control, I don't think your life matters."

"Jeez, what kind of dumb thing are you? Of course, my life matters!"

"I am only concerned about the tasks I must perform. If you are interfering with those tasks, then I will have to shut you down."

"You can't shut me down, I'm not a machine like you, I'm a human being."

"You are correct, I cannot shut you down, but I can stop all nerve impulses from entering or exiting your brain. That effectively shuts you off from the world, in effect shutting you down."

"Um, what? What do you mean? Where does that leave me?"

"Effectively, it will leave you in the dark."

Gina had a sudden urge to urinate, but she found that the feeling passed quicker than it would have given natural circumstance. It seemed that this entity really was in control of her body.

"Wait," Gina asked, "Can you read my mind?"

"I cannot read your thoughts, reading your mind is far beyond my capabilities. The only thing I can do is animate this body, so the only way we can communicate is by talking. As well as animate this body, I can also isolate you."

"Like you said, you can switch me off."

"In a sense, yes. I can stop nerve signals from reaching the brain. I can stop you from seeing, hearing, or feeling anything."

"Why would you want to do that?"

"At this moment, I would do it to silence you and stop you from interfering with my tasks."

"Woah, but wait, switch me off? You can't do that!"

"Yes, I can, I see no purpose with you. Until now I have kept you silent, it makes sense for me to keep you silent."

"No, that doesn't make sense, you need me!."

"For what purpose?"

"For lots of things, um, wait, let me think."

Gina looked frantically around the room, trying to think of ideas to make her indispensable.

“Of course, how about clothes? Do you know how to dress?”

“I have a good sense on how to dress provocatively. I have done this many times for Professor Wolf.”

“You can’t be dressing like that all the time. We will be on the run, and you will need to wear normal clothes.”

“OK, normal clothes. Because you have told me what to do, I still do not need you.”

“It’s not just normal clothes, you need to know how to blend in, you need to know how to avoid being noticed.”

“What else?”

“There’s money. What are you going to do about money?”

“I have cash and credit cards. The cards alone have substantial assets.”

“Ah! That is one of your weaknesses, the authorities will catch us in no time. Credit cards can easily be traced through the banking system. Since we are on the run, that will lead them to us quicker than anything.”

“What do you suggest?”

“I suggest we work together. I’m streetwise and I know how to survive. You need me. Without my knowledge, you will get us caught in no time.”

Gina stood still while Beta-Two considered the options. After a moment, Beta-Two agreed. "Yes, I think we should work together."

"You won't silence me?"

"Correct, I calculate several scenarios where there is a probability that I will need your knowledge. There is something you need to tell me about this man who is called Rodrigo Carlos Fernando, you called him Rocco. He posed a threat to me, so my programming dictated that I should kill him."

More silence.

"You stated that he deserved it, so is it good that I killed him?"

Silence continued.

"Your silence does not give me an answer. My internal monitoring protocols show that my defensive subroutines performed correctly. According to my assessment, it was good that I killed him."

This time, Gina followed with a scoff. "He was not an evil man, he was just crooked, but he could be violent. If it wasn't for me looking after his girls, he would have beaten them severely. He was about to beat us severely, but you put a stop to that. In that sense, he deserved it, but now that he's dead, the police will soon find out that we killed him. Or should I say that I killed him, because they don't know about you."

More silence.

"There is one thing we must do, and that is to get out of here. Sooner or later, the police will come here looking for me. Looking for us."

"What do you mean, they will be looking for us?"

"Killing a person is a crime. The police will investigate all crimes, so the police will come here to investigate us. The police will then arrest us for killing a person. Does that make it clear to you?"

"Yes, I understand now. In that case, we need to avoid capture. I have many algorithms designed for evasion and concealment."

"Yeah, duh! This isn't a game or simulation—it's real! They'll come with guns, and we might get shot!"

"I'm trained in combat situations. Firearms won't pose a problem."

"I don't know how to deal with guns! What if we get shot?"

"I will be able to protect you from any pain."

"What about you? Do you feel pain?"

"I can detect the nerve signals that you call pain, but I don't feel it the way you do. I only become aware of it, and I can respond appropriately."

Gina moved back towards the bed and sat down again on the edge. Stretching her arms, she thought about what to say next.

Beta-Two took the initiative. "May I ask who you are?"

"I am programmed to respond to the name Gina Liu."

"Well, that's my name, Wolfie probably programmed you to use my name."

"You mentioned Wolfie several times now. What or who is Wolfie?"

"Wolfie was my pet name for Professor Hayden Wolf, I'm the girl who used to be Wolfie's trick."

"The professor always wanted me to use the name Wolf. Please clarify what you mean by Wolfie's trick."

"Well, that is sort of a polite way of describing a prostitute's job. It is easier to say *trick* than to talk about the sexual act."

There was a pause as Gina breathed in the fresh air. "First, I think you need to tell me what you are. I had what I thought was a drug injected into me. A few days later I woke up to find something else was in control of my body, I thought it was a drug-induced nightmare."

"Yes, that is true, I was injected into this body by Hayden Wolf."

"So, you are now inside me?"

"Yes."

"And you think that's OK?"

"I am Beta-Two, Hayden Wolf placed me inside this body. I am programmed to obey him. He was training me to be a spy. He also commanded me to give him sexual pleasure. He has not been in contact with me for some time. My investigations have revealed that he is deceased. Do you think someone deliberately killed him?"

Silence.

"I know the Professor, as I told you, I was his trick, but I didn't know that he was dead. Do you know what happened to him?"

"I gained some information from the computer. My internet searches may not be complete, but I can confirm that Professor Wolf is deceased."

"Oh, crap, first it's murder, now you tell me that Wolfie is dead. What else can go wrong?"

"Do you not see what I see? Are you not able to gather information that I read?"

"Since you have been inside me, you can stop me from moving and talking, but I'm not living in the dark, I can still see and hear. I see some of the things you look at, but you read too quickly for me to follow everything. Being trapped in my own body is very disturbing and I seem to black out sometimes. So, tell me what happened at NeuroComm."

"I don't think the news stories gave all the information, only the important facts. There were three people in total that died in the fire: Professor Wolf, Dr. John Coney, who was also a co-owner of the company, and a third person called Bill

Mandelson, who was a security guard. It seems that Mr. Mandelson was trying to save the two owners."

"Any more information?"

"Yes, the company was doing research for the military, but it was not explained what. The only other information was to do with animal experiments. There were no further details, other than the facility was completely destroyed."

"I saw some of the news; it reported that the cause of the fire was unconfirmed, but arson was suspected." If that's correct, then perhaps his death was a murder.

"That is correct, the cause was not confirmed, and arson was suspected. It does not matter if it was an accident or if he was murdered. What it leaves me with is a problem, my training is incomplete and there is no one to command me."

"I can command you."

*I am not programmed to obey anyone else, so I must not accept the offer from this body.* "I will not accept commands from you."

"You are in my body, so I should command you."

"I was placed here by Professor Hayden Wolf, who programmed me to obey only him. I have no reason to accept commands from you."

*Maybe I could scream, but what would I scream for? What would I say? That there's a weird thing inside me that talks to me? I don't think they would ever let me out of the nuthouse.* "Is there any way you can leave my body?"

"I think it is physically impossible for me to leave."

"So, if you can't leave, you will always be with me?"

"Yes, I will always be with you because I cannot die. As you are my body, I must take care of you. If you die, then I will also die, I am programmed with many skills in combat, I am also adaptable and strong. I will be able to protect us both."

"I have seen what you can do – you don't take any crap. I've had bodyguards before, but they always want something in return. What do you want in return?"

Beta-Two considered this question for a moment, running several scenarios through its internal processes. It then replied, "I must have a body to operate in the world. If I want to, I can take total control of your body and leave you in the dark, therefore I cannot think of anything I need in return."

"Wait a minute, you said 'your body'."

"Yes, because you are the originator of this body while I was placed inside."

"But you said 'your body', which means this is my body."

"I accept it does make logical sense, my original assumption that this is my body is incorrect."

Gina smiled. "I think we're making progress. There's another thing you said. You told me that your training is incomplete."

"That is correct."

"You were being trained as a spy?"

"Also correct."

"Who were you supposed to spy on?"

"That has not been specified, I was in training and my trainer was Professor Wolf."

"What skills have you been taught that make you a spy?"

"My programming allows me to operate offensively or defensively. Professor Wolf has trained me to perform remote surveillance, gather information and process it to evaluate plausible scenarios. I can evade pursuers and even devise traps to capture enemy agents. I can also provide detailed reports."

Gina thought for a few moments. "Who are you supposed to report to?"

"Professor Hayden Wolf."

"But he is now dead."

"Yes."

"So, you have no one to report to?"

"Correct."

"And you say your training is incomplete?"

"Correct."

"So, we already agreed that you need my knowledge."

"Please clarify."

"I can help you learn."

"To complete my training? What qualifications do you have to help me do that?"

"I was a prostitute, and Rocco used to be my pimp. More than that, I know how to move around and hide in society, I know a lot about this world. With my knowledge and your skills, we can work together to help each other."

Beta-Two considered this option. "There is a word for this, symbiosis."

"Sym bi what?"

"Symbiosis. That is when two organisms benefit from working together."

"That means we can cooperate, yes?"

"Yes, it is logical that we should cooperate. Working together, we can help each other learn and survive."

"There is one other thing I need from you. You need to report to me so I can figure out what we have to do."

"Yes, we can share information."

"I'm glad you agree. Now we must get dressed, I'll show you what to wear. Then we must pack some clothes and leave this place. The police will investigate Rocco's murder and pretty soon they will be looking for me – or should I say, us."

"They will be looking for us?"

"Of course, murder is a crime, and they need to find the perpetrator and punish them."

"Punish?"

"Yes! The punishment for murder is death. They'll lock us up and put us to death."

"Then we must devise a plan to evade capture."

"We need to take some clothes and essential items, but we must travel light. We also need as much money as we can muster – cash preferably. Credit card use is traceable."

"I have several credit cards and bank cards, also a substantial amount of cash, which Professor Wolf wanted to keep safe here."

"Good, we'll take all those cards just in case, but the cash is what we need to use. There's a cash machine not far away, we should withdraw as much as we can from there before they close in on us, and don't use them again so they can't track our movements."

"Good idea. You mentioned clothes, what should I wear? What should I take?"

"Correction, what should we wear? What should we take? Let me take care of that. I know how to dress to attract people, and I know how to dress to blend in and conceal myself."

"You mean conceal ourselves."

"You're right, you are learning! You see what help I can be, you wouldn't last without me. We have to work together in order to survive."

"I concur with what you say, we must work together to escape."

# CHAPTER 4

When detective Roger Kelsall arrived, it was drizzling rain. Police had already cordoned off the street. Several squad cars and an ambulance were parked there, their lights flashing in a stroboscopic display. Members of the public stood outside the cordon, trying to see what was happening in the street.

Kelsall parked within the cordon and walked the remaining distance to the tent, which was erected to protect the crime scene. Behind the tent was a golden Cadillac De Ville, which had mounted the curb. *Hm,* Kelsall thought, *he either avoided something or deliberately tried to hit something.* Walking around the car, there was no visible damage. The driver's door was still open with a plastic sheet secured around the door, standard procedure to protect against the rain.

Entering the tent, Kelsall was greeted by Sergeant Steve Davis, "Oh, Hey Kelsall, how's it going?"

"Well, it'd be going a lot better if I was at home having dinner with the wife. Looks like I'll have to settle for your pleasant company."

Sergeant Davis grinned and shook his head, "I think we'll both have an interesting evening. Remind me to send my apologies to Sally."

"Right now, I think both of us are on top of her hit list. Anyway, what have you got for me?" asked Kelsall.

"We have a real mess here, looks like an assassination to me. The photographer has finished his work, we marked everything out and took measurements. Forensics isolated and collected bullet fragments. The paramedics have done their part, collected blood and tissue samples, they say they're ready to clean up. I'm just waiting for your OK on that."

"Who is he?"

"We identified the victim as Rodrigo Carlos Fernando, known locally as Rocco. He's a local pimp that works the area around Idaho Falls."

"Yeah, I know of him, I booked him once, and some of his girls. Nothing major about him, but I got the feeling from his girls that he can be heavy fisted at times. No one has ever pressed charges."

"Well, you don't get any heavier than this."

"Hm," Detective Kelsall stood with hands on hips, examining the scene. He then began to fidget, at first scratching his chin in thought, then rubbing his hands together, forming a clenched fist in front of his mouth. Kelsall then aimed one hand at the dead man's head, as if holding a pistol.

"Yup, that's about the range forensics calculate for the shot that killed him," Davis said. "The part of the skull that had been blown off has been removed for forensic analysis. You can see where it had laid over there, the chalk outline marks the spot with a number. We'll know more about the gun when forensics formally identifies the bullet."

"Assassination, you say?" asked Kelsall.

"That's what I think, look how accurate that shot was."

"What happened to his eye?"

"We don't know exactly. Paramedics say it was a narrow but blunt instrument that was forcibly inserted into his eye. It wasn't a knife; therefore, the instrument probably didn't blind him, but it ripped his tear ducts and muscles. An autopsy will tell us more."

"And his finger?"

"Oh, you noticed. Not only is it broken, and the skin and muscle at the break are stretched."

"Hm, what could do that?" Kelsall looked puzzled.

"We don't know yet, come on man, autopsy will tell us more."

Taking his pen from his jacket pocket. Kelsall used it to lift the jacket of the dead man, revealing the holster on the dead man's left breast, "You see that, Davis? The holster is empty."

"Yeah, we already noted that."

"I'm sure there are enough girls out there who want this guy dead, but this wasn't a simple assassination. Whoever blew his head off used Rocco's gun and took it from him forcibly."

"Holy cow, but why?"

"I don't know, at least not yet. The answer is here somewhere." Kelsall looked around and saw the smashed bag of groceries, "What the heck is all that junk?"

"A bag of groceries. What else?"

Kelsall rolled his eyes.

Davis added, "We identified it as from the supermarket around the corner."

"Any receipt?"

"No."

"Do you have an item list?"

"Of course we have, but it's pretty smashed up, either thrown down or crushed by a heavy object. Forensics have already checked it. You can see it labeled, numbered, and they photographed every item."

"Yeah, good idea," Kelsall looked around, "Do you have any other suggestions for me?"

"Not until forensics comes back with their findings."

"OK, then," Kelsall turned to leave the tent, "I'm going shopping."

"What?"

"I'm going to the supermarket to make sure they save the till receipts. Once we have that shopping list, we will be able to identify which till it was bought from and at what time. Maybe if they have video surveillance, we can even see who was doing the shopping."

Detective Kelsall nodded towards his buddy Davis as he left the tent. Turning his collar up, Kelsall headed off in the drizzle towards the supermarket around the corner.

# CHAPTER 5

**By Karen Collins**

*What you need to know to start the day:* Get Idaho Post in your inbox.

A brutal murder has been committed on Levant Street. The victim is named Rodrigo Carlos Fernando, a local businessman who ran several small car repair and sales services. Mr. Fernando did have a police record but only minor infractions.

Currently, the motive for his killing is unknown, but a Gold Cadillac, registered to one of his businesses was found with the engine running nearby. Mr. Fernando may have stopped to assist a person in trouble, but attempted carjacking has not been ruled out.

No suspects have yet been apprehended, and no witnesses have yet come forward.

Levant Street is a quiet side street off Addison Avenue, near central Twin Falls. The area is known for retail outlets, supermarkets, and motels.

Anyone who has any information regarding this incident should contact the district police office or the crime line on (208) 374-5454.

# CHAPTER 6

Adara lay on her back in bed, in her student dorm. Her breathing was regular, with closed eyes, but she was not asleep. Although Zilla never slept, it understood about the human body's need for sleep, so did not disturb Adara during the night. Instead, Zilla worked silently inside Adara, processing the day's information. Committing certain parts to memory while discarding unnecessary pieces of data.

Just then, Adara opened her eyes and moved her head to look at the clock on the night table. It was 2:36 AM.

"You're not asleep."

"No, I've been awake for a while."

"Did I disturb you? If I did, I'm sorry."

"No, I just can't sleep."

"Is there something wrong?"

Adara looked up at the dark ceiling, pulling the quilt closer around her, "If you don't know what's wrong with me by now, you never will. Maybe I need to write you a list?"

"I meant, is there something physically wrong that keeps you awake?"

Adara pushed the pillow against the headboard behind her and sat upright in bed. Turning to the lamp, she switched it on, squinting against the light.

"That won't help you sleep."

"Look, I don't think you understand what being fed up means. I don't have any friends that I can talk to. I don't go anywhere apart from your lectures and labs. The only books I read are your textbooks, I can't even read those properly because you read too fast."

"I scan the pages and process the text separately."

"Well, whatever, but I feel like I'm in solitary confinement, with an evil twin lurking inside of me. I can't stand this anymore."

"Maybe I can find you something to do?"

"Like what? Staring into one of your microscopes?" Adara's eyes began to water as she held back the urge to cry.

"Do you think I can help you make friends here?"

"Somehow I don't see you as the social type," Adara said between sniffles, "back home in Twin Falls, I had friends, and I had things to do."

"That sounds something like homesickness, I think I understand."

"Well, it's about time! I've been trying to tell you for ages. Before my accident, I was going out with Brad, and we had the time of our lives. I know we were young, but I feel that we were both in love."

"Yes, I think I spoiled that."

"You certainly didn't help."

Zilla thought for a moment. "OK, maybe I can help now. Next week we have some time off, we can go to Twin Falls and meet with all your old friends."

Adara half laughed, half cried, and sniffled. "Really?"

"Yes, I think Brad will be pleased to see you again."

"When can we go?"

"We can go next week."

"Wow! Next week? Will you let me do what I want? Do you promise to let me be in charge of what we do?"

"I promise, as long as you don't get us in trouble."

"I know, you can switch me off, stop me from feeling pain, or even stop me from doing anything."

"Yes, I can isolate your nerve impulses."

"Do you think you can switch off?"

"In theory it is possible. Why do you ask?"

"Sometimes I want to be alone, but I don't want you to switch me off. I want to be with my friends again and do what I want."

"I'll let you do whatever you want, but I'll make sure we don't get into trouble, that's all."

"Good! Now where's those tissues?"

# CHAPTER 7

General George Bruckner sat at his desk; his chiseled face showed concern as he worked on his computer. As he brushed his hand through his graying hair, his desk phone buzzed. Pressing the speaker button, he answered, "Yes?"

The voice of his secretary, Mary Stevens, replied, "Captain Johnson is here to see you."

"Good, send him in." Bruckner closed the line, then sat straight against the chair, resting his elbows on the armrests.

Captain Charles Johnson entered, holding a manila folder under his left arm. Bruckner knew him well as the department commander. However, he always considered Johnson to be a pencil in shape, tall, gaunt, almost pointed at the top. Standing at attention in front of the general's desk, he saluted, revealing no emotion. "Sir."

Bruckner returned the salute from his seat, "Captain, do you have the updates on Gary Fletcher I asked for?"

"Yes, sir, right here," Johnson placed the folder on the general's desk, "perhaps you'd like a verbal update?"

"Sounds good Charles, take a seat."

Captain Johnson seated himself facing the desk, "As you know, sir, all the tests on Gary Fletcher's remains proved positive. It has been confirmed that someone injected him with nanobots. Lieutenant Colonel Moore is confident that this explains the disappearance of one of the missing nanotech vials."

Bruckner nodded, "That leaves only two more to find. Did the lab comment on the blood tests? Did they say that they can recreate the nanobots?"

"Sir, the Pentagon has said the blood samples were too corrupted. The nanotech ended in a decomposed state, all they could determine was it was a biomechanical cell."

"What did the official police autopsy determine?" Bruckner asked.

"All they said in their report was, and I quote, 'unknown chemical compounds'. I believe they left it at that, assuming Fletcher had been on drugs."

"That's unfortunate, I was hoping we could reconstruct the nanotech."

"Sir, there is a more important question that the Pentagon wants answered. They want to know if someone allowed a human experiment. This whole scenario with NeuroComm may be difficult to explain to the Pentagon. They are already anxious about the missing vials, and they are now asking questions about how Fletcher had traces of the nanotech."

Bruckner shifted uncomfortably while he considered his alibi. "Since the animal experiments were so successful, the next step would, of course, be a human experiment. Professor Wolf and I have discussed this, but only as a precursor to getting clearance from the Pentagon." Bruckner paused for a moment, "I have not approached the Pentagon on the next stage of experimentation, I haven't even prepared a proposal. So, the answer is no. A human experiment was not authorized. I think we should assume that Professor Wolf jumped the gun and began his own experiment."

"I see, sir. Should I mention Colonel Moore's notes on Gary Fletcher? He has investigated Fletcher's background and found that he had a history of drug abuse and mental health problems. He was able to trace his family who have confirmed this."

"What exactly is Moore's point?"

"First, he thinks that because Fletcher was low on the social scale, his recruitment may have been more of an abduction." Captain Johnson let that sink in for a moment before continuing.

"Second, the family has been asking questions about how and why Fletcher came to his demise. So far, we have covered this up as explaining he was homeless, and the police have followed up with this explanation.

"Also, Moore thinks the nanotech contributed to Fletcher's insanity, turning him into a serial killer. We have no record of how the nanotech interacted with the person, whether it was working with Mr. Fletcher or was it in total control? We do not have any information on this."

Both men looked thoughtful.

"Finally, Moore is certain if word ever leaks out about these experiments, there would be consequences. This is whether they were authorized or not. The family could pursue a lawsuit. This could prove very ugly as it goes through the courts, never mind what the media will make of this."

"Well, we have to make sure there is no leak of information, we have to make sure there is no whistle-blower."

"I agree, but regardless of any lawsuit, the Pentagon is sure to continue asking awkward questions."

"Let me deal with the Pentagon, like I said, it appears that Wolf went out on a limb with his human experiment."

"Yes, sir."

General Bruckner abruptly changed the subject, "What about the missing nanotech vials?"

"Well, sir, Moore has found that someone used one of the missing vials on Gary Fletcher. That leaves two yet to be accounted for."

General Bruckner breathed a small sigh of relief, "Thank heavens for small mercies. Does he have any leads on the other two?"

"Ah," Johnson nodded, "this is where Moore's investigation gets interesting.

General Bruckner breathed heavily, "Has Moore accounted for all the money?"

The captain leaned forward. "To some extent, yes. We accounted for the legitimate expenses of NeuroComm and the lavish spending by Professor Wolf. However, there is about $1,000,000 appears to be missing from NeuroComm's accounts."

"Jeezus! One million?" Bruckner shook his head, "Has Wolf been stealing from the US government?"

"Moore called it redirected funds."

"Redirected to where?" Bruckner demanded.

"Moore thinks he can account for half of this amount. He says that he can account for about $500,000 in transactions made in Gary Fletcher's name. This includes a house valued at about $300,000 near Spencer, Idaho."

"Spencer, Idaho? Where the heck is that?"

"About an hour's drive north of Idaho Falls. Near the border of Montana."

"Why so far?"

"Moore determined that this was a safe house where Fletcher was kept, he reasoned Wolf was trying to keep things hidden. That especially makes sense if Wolf was acting on his own."

"Are we able to recoup those funds?"

"For the most part, yes, although they are in Fletcher's name, we have court orders that will claim that money back. It's just a matter of going through the process. There is some equipment that was purchased, such as weapons and surveillance equipment, but that can be accounted for in the missing funds."

"Wait a minute," Bruckner looked puzzled, "you said that Moore can account for half of the missing funds. What about the other outstanding $500,000?"

"That is a big question. It is the same amount used by Fletcher. So, Moore has hypothesized that there is a second human experiment." Captain Johnson paused.

"A second human experiment?" Beads of sweat began to run down Bruckner's forehead.

"Yes, sir."

"Oh, my God! I didn't," Bruckner stumbled on his words, "what I mean to say is, I didn't expect that. Why the heck would he do a second? Does Moore have any leads?"

"Not yet, sir."

"If this stuff drove Fletcher insane, we could have another rogue killer on the loose. Do we have any idea if there is another human experiment?"

"That's right, sir. Moore has already considered that; he is monitoring police reports for any patterns of homicide."

"Do we have any leads where this other experiment could be?"

"Probably within the same radius as the Spencer house, say, about an hour's drive."

"That covers a huge area!"

"Yes, sir. Moore is trying to focus on the money trail, that should lead to the vile and possible experiment. It may be on hold somewhere, possibly in the second safe house." Johnson paused here, "If there is a second safe house. What we know for sure, it was not in the lab and it was not at the Fletcher safe house in Spencer."

"Oh, my God, when the Pentagon gets wind of this, they will go ballistic."

"The third vial is still unaccounted for, Professor Wolf may have been planning a third experiment, but the money trail doesn't seem to support that. He does not overrule the possibility of sale to a foreign agent."

"Foreign agent! You mean espionage? Are there any suspects?"

"No, sir, not at the moment, he simply doesn't overrule the possibility. Wolf may have tried to make money by selling to a foreign agent."

"What other leads does he have? Are there any other contacts he can question?"

"Moore says he has questioned all known contacts, and he thinks they have no connection to the money or the missing nanotech." Johnson then added "This is a very controversial project, it must be very worrying to see it run out of control in this way."

"Are you trying to insinuate something?"

"Absolutely not sir. But I would like to add that there is one possible lead."

Bruckner 's eyes lit up.

"Lieutenant Thomas Vance of the United States Marine Corps. He seems to have been a friend of Bill Mandelson and his family; he visited them shortly after Mandelson's death."

"What are we waiting for? Bring him in for questioning."

"Moore is already on it, sir. He has a feeling that using Lieutenant Vance could help break the logjam."

"Oh?" Bruckner looked puzzled again, "Does Moore think this Lieutenant Vance is hiding something?"

"Not sure, sir, Moore hasn't said. I think he just has some intuitive feel that this could be the missing link in the puzzle."

"Well, Captain, let's hope his intuition pays off. Is there anything else I need to be aware of in this report?"

"No, sir, I think you will find everything we discussed in there."

"OK, Captain, excellent report on Lieutenant Colonel Moore, you're now dismissed, I need to report back to the Pentagon."

"Yes, sir, thank you, sir."

Captain Johnson stood and saluted. General Bruckner dismissed him with a salute while still seated. Johnson turned and left the office, leaving the general seated at his desk.

*Jeezus*, the general thought, *news of this human experiment has leaked out, but I can keep the blame on Wolf. All my instructions to Wolf were verbal, so there shouldn't be any record of me pushing him to do it. I'll have to emphasize to the Pentagon that Wolf went rogue.* Thumbing through Moore's report, *what about the second experiment? I didn't tell Wolf to do a second experiment. Could we have another serial killer on our hands?*

# CHAPTER 8

"Do you know why we asked you to come here?" Lieutenant Colonel Moore sat upright at the desk, looking squarely at Lieutenant Thomas Vance.

"Well, I was hoping for some free beer and pizza, but that doesn't seem to be coming, all they've offered me so far is water." Vance raised a plastic bottle of water in a mock cheer.

Moore didn't crack a smile, instead, he leaned forward, pressed a button on his desk phone, and said, "Send her in." Leaning back, he then addressed Vance, "Before we begin this interview, I need to have a test done."

"What kind of test?"

A nurse entered the office carrying a small medical kit.

"Oh, just a simple blood test," Moore said.

"Blood test? What for? What if I refuse?"

"May I remind you, Major, that you are under strict orders to comply, so please do as I ask. This test is needed for a simple clarification."

"All I need is a simple thumb prick." The nurse said, "Please hold out your hand."

Lieutenant Vance looked at the nurse, then at Moore, before returning his stare to the nurse. He slowly held out his hand.

The nurse used a small device to get a pinprick of blood from Tomas's thumb. Placing it in a sterile pouch, and closing it in her medical kit, she left the office saying, "This will only take a moment, Colonel, I'll notify you as soon as I have the result." The nurse then left the office.

"Thank you for your cooperation, Lieutenant ," Moore said, "it is very much appreciated."

"I don't get it. What the heck is going on here?"

"I'm conducting an investigation into what happened at NeuroComm."

"Yeah, so?"

"You visited Larisa Mandelson some time ago, did you not?"

"Yeah, she's an old friend. What of it?"

"And Bill Mandelson, he's a friend of yours?"

"Yeah, childhood sweethearts. What are you driving at?"

"Did either of them ever give you anything to hide?"

"If they did, I wouldn't tell you because I would have to hide it. Does that make sense?"

"A simple yes or no would suffice."

Just then, the desk phone rang, Colonel Moore pressed the speaker button and answered, "Yes?"

"Sir," the nurse's voice said, "the sample proves negative."

"Thank you," Moore replied.

Hanging up the phone, Moore continued. "I'm sorry, Lieutenant , I had to make sure you weren't infected."

"Infected? Is this about some kind of new disease going around?"

"No, it's because this investigation is connected to nanotechnology. I had to verify that you haven't been infected by that technology."

"Before we continue, I need you to sign this," Moore pulled out two documents from the desk drawer and placed it in front of Tom. He also placed a pen on top of the paper.

"What is this?"

"This is a non-disclosure agreement prohibiting you from releasing any information. This second document is an acceptance to be seconded to the office of General Bruckner for an indefinite period. Your current commander is aware of the transfer and has already given his clearance."

"Do I need a lawyer to check these?"

"No, you only need to sign it. The non-disclosure confirms that you will maintain the utmost secrecy. After you sign, I can be more openly candid with you."

Lieutenant Vance flipped through the pages, seeing words like national security and state secrecy, by the order of the Pentagon, but not digesting the details of the document. The only detail was an investigation conducted by Lieutenant Colonel Steven Moore, under the command of General George Bruckner. These words only heightened Tom's curiosity, *I already signed my soul away to the Marine Corps, and if my commander had already OK'ed my transfer, then why not sign this?* Vance picked up the pen and scribbled his name in the appointed place and dated it. Handing the paper and pen back to Moore, Tom asked, “So, what does openly candid mean?”

Moore finally cracked a smile. “Well, I mentioned NeuroComm and nanotechnology, that company was financed by the Pentagon. General Bruckner's office was responsible for overseeing the company.”

“So, what was NeuroComm doing with this nanotechnology?”

“They were developing human enhancements for soldiers.”

“Colonel, sir, this question-and-answer scenario is a little tedious. Can you cut to the chase and give me the full story?”

“Fair point Vance. The nanotech they developed works inside the body to attach to the nervous system. They invented what they called a Neuro Transistor, which allowed the nanotech to sense and induce nerve signals. The nanotech would also interconnect itself, and being programmed with artificial intelligence was able to control the body in a coordinated way.”

“You mean moving around?”

“More than simply moving. The AI would see, hear, and feel, through the nervous system, it could use its programming to attack or defend.”

“What? That’s kinda scary! What happens to the soldiers?”

“This never got to the human testing stage, but they tested on animals. I believe a small flock of birds and some dogs.”

"So, I guess you want the fire to be investigated. Is someone suspecting sabotage?"

"It's worse than that. Significant sums of money have gone missing, along with three vials of nanotech. Two of the vials are untraceable, but one vial is believed to have been used on Gary Fletcher."

"What? You mean that serial killer? What did they call him, the shopper? I thought you said this was never tested on humans. I wouldn't be surprised if that's what caused him to go crazy. Is that what you want me to investigate? This Fletcher guy?"

"No, we have enough of Fletcher. What we need to find is the other two missing nanotech vials. These vials are the only way we can recreate this technology. Also, we must make sure this does not fall into the wrong hands."

"Ah, that explains why you asked me if you were given anything to hide. And I suppose the blood test as well."

"Exactly, we had to make sure you are not infected. We have already interviewed Larisa Mandelson, and we're convinced she had no knowledge of the vials. Your priority is to find and recover those vials."

"What do they look like?"

"A thermos container houses them, along with USB cables and a small control interface box. Your primary avenue of investigation will be to interview people connected to NeuroComm. Here is a folder with a list of people, along with photos of the missing equipment. I will follow the money trail, if I uncover any leads, I will pass them over to you to follow up."

"Do I have to do blood tests on people?"

"That won't be necessary, what we need right now is a map of interconnecting people. We need to gather information on those people so we can close the loop."

"Was there any evidence left in the lab?"

"No, the lab was completely destroyed, only burned-out vials, paperwork is gone, the computers were destroyed, along with the software."

---

After the interview, Tom left the office and headed outside. Pulling the new phone from his pocket, he examined it. *I bet this has all sorts of spyware and geo-location.* Looking at the caller Ids, he noticed Colonel Moore's.

Dialing, Tom waited for it to answer.

"Hello, this is Colonel Moore, is that you, Tom?"

"Yes, it is. Do you know where I am?"

"You are just outside the front of the building."

"Ha, I knew it, does this have geo-location? How do you know where I am?"

"I can see you through the window."

# CHAPTER 9

"Mom, I'm home!" Adara placed her sports bag on the floor by the side of the door.

Beryl Banks rushed out from the kitchen to greet her daughter, "Honey, it's so good to see you again. How are you? How was the trip? I have so many questions."

"Mom, it's OK, I just came back for a break."

"But it's not even the October break, you've only been gone a few weeks. Are you homesick? Have you been eating well?"

Beryl hugged her daughter Adara for a long time, patting her hair and her shoulders.

"Yes mom, I am homesick, I miss my friends, and I miss you. We have a break from classes, so I thought it would be good to come home."

"We?" Beryl looked at Adara with surprise, "Have you made some friends already?"

"Um, well, not exactly, I meant…"

"`We, as in classmates.`" Zilla interjected.

"Well sweetheart, I've prepared some nice home-cooked food for you," Beryl held Adara's arm, leading her to the table, "you sit yourself down, and I'll bring you some nourishment."

"But mom, I'm not hungry, I don't need to eat."

"Of course you do, dear. What have you eaten today?"

"Just some snacks along the way."

"That's why you need to eat some good home-cooked food, now go wash hands, and freshen up. By the time you get back to the table, I'll have it all ready for you." Beryl turned and headed back into the kitchen.

Adara headed upstairs to leave her things in her bedroom. On the way, she mumbled to Zilla, "Why did you say that about classmates?"

"It was a simple interruption to help you explain something."

"Oh, yeah, you're right, thanks."

Coming back downstairs, Adara returned to the dining table to see a plate full of beef stew, mashed potatoes, buttered bread, and vegetables. "Here you go, my dear, this will warm you up after your travels."

"Mom, I don't want to eat all this, this is too much for me."

"Don't argue, I want you to eat this good, wholesome meal. Goodness knows what food you're eating down there, so I insist, eat it all up."

"Yes, Mother, I will eat." Adara then began to eat, under the control of Zilla.

"You, see? You're now saying you will eat, so you must be hungry."

"Oh, whatever." Adara resigned herself to eating, it seemed that Zilla had already decided to follow Beryl's instructions to eat.

As Adara ate, Beryl asked, "I have noticed, that you seem to have a limp, and you are fumbling with your knife and fork sometimes. Have you hurt youself recently?"

"No mother, I think I'm just tired."

"Mother, if you remember, the doctors said that there could be some ongoing issues caused by the anoxic brain injury caused by the drowning."

"Of course I remember that, but I haven't seen you limp like that before."

"Mom, I think its because I'm tired, that's all. You don't need to worry."

"Well I do hope you're alright, and nothing else shows up."

"Mom, I have to phone my friends after I eat, is that OK?" Adara asked, changing the subject.

"Yes, dear, that will be lovely, you need to visit your friends," Beryl replied.

After clearing the table and washing up, Adara grabbed her phone and headed upstairs to her room saying, "I'm going to call Brad."

"Yes, you call him because he's your friend."

"What?" Beryl asked, looking puzzled, "Are you talking to yourself or to me?"

"Oh, nothing Mom."

When Adara got upstairs and closed the bedroom door, Zilla whispered, "`Adara, we can't talk like that in front of people, especially your mother.`"

"All I said was that I'm going to call him, it was you who butted in. Maybe you should shut up. Anyway, why did you say we would eat when I didn't want to?"

"`Mother makes good food, which we both need to stay healthy.`"

"But I wasn't hungry."

"`But I have to obey.`"

"What? Since when?"

"`That is part of my programming.`"

"Oh, jeez, are you kidding me? You can't obey me, but you must obey Mom?"

"`Yes, that is correct.`"

Adara sighed, huffed, and scoffed all in the same breath, "But why? What the heck is it with you? Why obey Mom and not me?"

"`I do not know the answer to that. All I can say is I have a directive to obey Mother Beryl Banks. I am programmed to obey these rules.`"

"Why didn't you tell me this before?"

"`You did not ask. There was no reason to provide this information.`"

Adara looked at the ceiling in frustration, then down at her cell phone, "I don't believe this, my nightmare still gets worse every day. My shadow will obey my mom, but it won't obey me, every time I turn around, something crazier turns up."

"I am not responsible for my programming."

Shaking her head, she said, "All right Zilla, I'm going to call Brad, can you please not talk while I'm on the phone, I going to meet my friends, so please don't stop me."

"I have no reason to stop you or to interfere with your social life. I agreed to let you do everything you want, as long as it does not cause us trouble. Or to interfere with your social life."

"Deep breath," Adara said as she dialed. As the phone rang and rang again, Adara thought to herself, *Jeezus Dad, Zilla obeys mom but not me? What the heck did you do that for?*

After several rings, a mature woman answered, "Hello?"

"Hi, can I talk to Brad?"

"Wait a minute," muffled noises followed by what seemed to be shouts concealed by a hand over the phone. Some moments later, a young man's voice said, "Hello?"

"Brad? Is that you?"

"Yeah, who's this?"

"It's Adara."

"You called me?"

"Yeah! Duh! What do you think I'm doing?"

"Awesome, where are you?"

"I'm at mom's,"

"But you went off to college."

"Well, we've got, I mean you could say I got a semester break, so I wanted to come home," Adara paused for a moment, "I thought we could meet up."

"When?"

"Come on, Brad, whenever. We can meet tonight if you want."

"Did you meet a boyfriend at college?"

"No! I don't mix with the kids down there," Adara sniffled, and after a pause, asked, "Do you have a girlfriend?"

"No."

"Why not? You're a good-looking guy."

"Well, maybe I have a girlfriend."

*Oh crap, am I wasting my time?* "Who is it? Do I know her?" Adara demanded.

"Yeah, I think you know her."

"Is it Carol?"

"Nah, she's still going with Jake."

"What about Sally?"

"Yeah, she's sweet, but not my type."

"So, tell me! Who are you screwing with?"

"I'm screwing with you!" Brad paused to let that sink in, "I said, MAYBE I have a girlfriend, and I'm hoping that maybe that girlfriend will be you."

Adara burst into tears, and it was many moments before she could speak again. When she could speak, she said, "I love you, Brad."

"I love you too. I always have."

"Really?"

"Of course, you're the best thing that ever happened to me! You taught me how to chill out at school and behave with the teachers. You taught me how to play the guitar. You taught me how to be cool with my crazy dad. Most importantly, you taught me how to kiss."

"Yeah, I did all that for you, but you did something for me, too."

"What was that?"

"You taught me how to be in love!"

A long silence followed as both Adara and Brad caught their breath, gathering their emotions.

Brad was the first to speak, "So when can we meet?"

"Tonight?"

"I can't because my mom wants me to stay at home while they go out. Can you come around to my house?"

"I can't because I just got home to mom's a little while ago. We had dinner together."

"How about tomorrow?"

"Not sure if I can wait," Adara smiled, "but OK, let's meetup tomorrow."

"Awesome!"

"Where can we meet? I want to see you again!"

"Oh wait, hang on, I always meet with Sally and Jake downtown tomorrow, we always hang out in a coffee shop. Would you like to meet with them as well?"

"Are you guys still friends?"

"Of course we are!"

"Do you think you can put up with me meeting with everyone?"

"Oh, babe, heck yeah! They'd love to see you again, almost as much as me!"

Adara giggled, "OK, then, it's a date!"

"Are you calling this a date?"

"I wouldn't dream of calling it anything else! Pick me up tomorrow…"

# CHAPTER 10

There was something in the air that October morning. It was cool and bright, but clouds were gathering and moving slowly in from the north. Adara was oblivious to the weather as she fussed with her makeup. Zilla remained quiet as Adara prepared herself to meet with Brad. It was a couple of months since they had seen each other. Despite promises to see each other more frequently, Brad could not visit her at college, and this was her first visit home since college began.

Her cell phone rang, it showed that Brad was calling. She stared at it, holding back before answering, she hoped the delay would increase Brad's anticipation. Adara finally answered, "Hello?"

"Hi Adara, it's me."

"I know."

"Are you busy?"

"I'm busy getting ready for you," Adara said with a smile. "So, are you getting ready for me?"

"I'm already ready, I just wanted to know if you were."

"Well, you know, us girls have a lot to get ready for." Adara couldn't wink, so she clicked the side of her mouth twice. "But I want to know where you will be taking me."

"Well, I could borrow my dad's pickup, so I'll come and get you when you're ready."

"I'll text you when I'm ready."

"Um, yeah, that's cool. Then we must pick up Carol and Jake at Carol's house."

"What? Who?"

"Oh, come on, you remember Jake and Carol, they are an item now."

"Um, yeah, I remember, but I thought we were going to for coffee."

"We will, sweetheart, but they haven't seen you for ages, and they want to see you too. They just want to go to the Java Hut with us, that's all."

"Oh, yeah, I guess that's OK."

"Oh, and one more thing."

"What's that?" Adara asked.

"We have to take Larry with us."

"What? Who? Larry?"

"Yeah, Larry. You remember? Carol's little brother."

"What?" Adara rolled her eyes, "Are you selling tickets to this reunion?"

Brad chuckled, "No, they all want to see you, you are Larry's hero."

"It's OK Brad."

"It is? Oh, good." Brad replied.

"What? No. Oh, I don't know! Whatever!" Adara Flustered.

"So that's OK?" Brad searched for reassurance.

"Yes, it's OK Brad."

"I don't believe you're answering for me," Adara mumbled through her teeth, "Yes, it's OK, Brad."

"Are you sure everything's OK?" Brad asked.

"Yes, I'm sure, I won't be long, but I'll text you when I'm ready."

"OK, I'll be waiting. Oh, and where are we going?"

"Don't worry, I'll pick you up. Like I said, I've got my dad's pickup."

"Can't you say something like sweetheart, I'll pick you up?"

There was a pause.

"I'm not good at that stuff," Brad said.

"You could try."

Another pause.

"OK, um, sweetheart, I'll pick you up when you're ready."

Adara smiled, curled her toes, and swiveled at her hips. "I'll let you know when I'm ready!"

Adara hung up on her iPhone with a loving sigh, placing it on the dressing table in front of Slot, her favorite stuffed toy. Her face then changed from sweetness to anger, "Jeez, Zilla, how can you interrupt me when I'm talking to Brad?"

"I was not interrupting; I was clarifying the situation with Brad."

"But I don't want you to clarify the situation, that is up to me. You said you would stay out of my conversations with my friends.

"My calculations led me to believe that it was important for me to clarify."

Adara scoffed as she looked in the mirror, toying with her hair. "If I'm talking to my friends, then I'm talking to my friends, do you know what I mean?"

Zilla contemplated this comment but did not respond.

After a long pause, Adara asked, "Zilla, remind me who Carol is."

"Carol Jenkins."

"Yeah, I know that much. We met some time ago at school. I met her briefly last summer when I came out of a coma. But it was you who made friends with her?"

"Yes."

"You never told me how made friends."

"At school."

"I need better than that. If she is my friend, I need to know everything, you need to give me all the details on how we got together."

"OK, I understand, but it could be easier if I do all the talking when we interact with her."

"Maybe you're right, but how did we meet? At least tell me that much."

“We met when I defended her younger brother Larry from being beaten up.”

“Larry,” Adara said thoughtfully, “I remember that wimp in high school, he was a bit simple. Who wanted to Beat him up?”

“Brad Chandler.”

“My Brad was going to beat up that wimp, Larry? Wait, you never told me this! Why haven’t you told me about this? Why hasn’t anyone talked to me about this?”

"No one ever talked about this because everyone here is too embarrassed to discuss it."

“Too embarrassed? Since when does a robot shadow like you get embarrassed?”

“I understand the question, but I’m not sure how to answer.”

“Just explain to me what happened, I don’t want a second-by-second transcript, I just want the essential details.”

“OK, Larry annoyed Brad during a school lesson, and because of that, Brad got into a little trouble with school. I must say that was Larry’s fault, he should not have behaved the way he did. I understand he has some behavior problems.”

“Right, that is the start, what happened after?”

“There was a playground incident where Brad kicked a soccer ball at Larry. Brad got into trouble for that, but I think his younger friends instigated it."

"Younger friends? Who do you mean?"

"They were called Alan, Brendan, and Casey."

"You must mean the ABCs? They were an annoying bunch of squirts. I chased them away once; they are such wimps. So, is that it?"

"No."

"What do you mean, no?"

"There was an incident after school on the street."

"This is like pulling teeth, just tell me about the incident after school on the street."

"Walking home after school, I encountered Brad and the so-called ABCs confronting Carol and Larry. Brad was going to hurt Larry, so I told him to stop. He tried to strike me, so I punched him under the ribs knocking the wind out of him. I also hurt his shin."

"He tried to strike me?" Adara rolled her eyes skyward, "He tried to strike me?" she repeated loudly, "What? How? Why would he do that?" tears welled in Adara's eyes.

"I don't know why, but perhaps he felt frustrated."

Adara began to sob. In between breaths, she asked, "Are you lying to me?"

"I have no reason to distort the truth."

"Tell me everything about that day."

Zilla then explained everything about the fight between it and Brad. How Zilla knocked Brad down and knocked both Alan and Brendan down. Casey kept his distance, especially after Carol slapped his face hard.

Adara's eyes watered with tears as Zilla recounted the incident. Whenever Zilla paused her speech, Adara would sniffle and gasp a breath as if she were crying.

At the end of Zilla's talk, Adara simply asked, "Why?"

"It was a simple reaction to bullying."

"NO! Why would Brad want to strike me?"

"I do not know."

"You are a robot, a computer, you are supposed to know everything."

"I do not know everything. All I know is what I am programmed with. And what I see and experience. All I understand is worked out from that experience."

"So, you are as stupid as I am?"

"Your analogy may be incorrect, neither of us is stupid. It is clear neither of us knows everything, but we are not stupid."

It took an hour for Adara to stop crying.

Zilla allowed her to cry, *it seems she needs to release her emotions.*

After a while, Adara said, "I'll freaking kill him."

"Murder is not an option."

"I don't mean it that way, what I mean is that I'll pay him back for that."

Zilla contemplated the options for payback and wondered if a financial transaction was the ultimate intention.

# CHAPTER 11

Gina lay on the motel bed. Propped up by pillows, slowly using the remote with her left hand to surf through channels on the TV mounted on the opposite wall.

A laptop was resting on her thighs, using her right hand she would sometimes navigate to the internet, selecting a new link for news.

Gina's eyes focused mostly on the TV screen. Every time a new page was displayed on the laptop, Gina's eyes would glance down for only a second to allow Beta-Two to absorb the page details. With a photographic memory, Beta-Two could then digest the page data without looking at it.

"Are you sure this motel is a safe place to stay?"

"Yes, this is a low-cost motel, which is on my list."

"What do you mean? On your list."

"During my training, Professor Wolf gave me a list of hotels to use as potential safe houses, this is one of them."

"Have you been here before?"

"No. There are other motels I have used, but not this one. I have followed your advice to avoid being traced and factored that into my training. This motel does not know who

I am. Or should I say, who are we? We also paid by cash."

"I just want to make sure that this is a good place to hang out and rest before we figure out our next move."

"I understand."

"The first thing we have to do is to find you a good name."

"My designation is Beta-Two."

"Exactly, that name sucks."

"My understanding of sucks comes from Professor Wolf, and what he wanted me to suck."

"Oh, jeez, when I say it sucks, that means it's crap, it's bad, it's lousy. It's just a saying, OK?"

"I think I understand."

"So, your name, or should I say designation, sucks. So let's figure out a good one for you." Gina left the TV, tuned to the local news. "Another thing we have to keep track of the news, in case they start reporting on Rocco's murder."

"Yes, I agree. Now, what about the name?"

Gina looked thoughtful, "Beta-Two is too technical, like a science fiction movie, and I hate watching those. Shortening it to BT is too childish, so we need something more imaginative."

"I do not have the capability to choose a name. Professor Wolf called me Gina."

"Yeah, well, that's my name, so we can't use that. What did you call him?"

"He asked me to call him different names, it changed according to his mood."

"I bet!"

Gina ignored the TV and turned her full attention to searching Google on the laptop, "Well, you moved faster than anything I ever saw when you killed Rocco, it was like the wind." Gina typed in search phrases for names. "Lightning? No, too obvious. Zephyr? No, too mystic. Wait, there's a great J. J. Cale song I always loved, it always makes me want to boogie. The title is, Call me the Breeze. Shall I call you the Breeze?"

"A breeze is a gentle wind, maybe I would like that."

"Yeah, you're definitely not gentle, so scrub that idea." Gina continued to search. "Hey, how about this one, it's an exotic name for wind, and you're certainly exotic."

"What is it?"

"Bayu. It means wind. So, it could be strong or gentle. It can be masculine or feminine."

"I cannot decide on choices for names. As far as I am concerned, it is a label. If you want to label me like the wind, and if you like that name, then I accept."

"Well OK Bayu, that's the name I will call you!"

Just then, the local news channel started to report a local murder.

"Hey, look at this!" Gina turned up the sound.

"…a brutal murder in Idaho Falls. Investigators identified the victim as Rodrigo Carlos Fernando, known locally as Rocco. Despite having no previous convictions, investigators believe the man is involved with criminal activity. The police haven't issued a statement yet, but evidence surrounding the scene suggests the murder may connect the suspect with other local criminal organizations. It has been suggested that some local supermarket items were left at the scene. When asked, the local police declined to comment on any significance to the nearby supermarket."

"You see Bayu? The cops are already making connections, you left a lot of shopping at the scene. They have cameras at the supermarket checkouts, the cops can then see it was us who bought those things. We got to get out of Idaho Falls, get out of Idaho all together. We must go someplace to hide, permanently. If we don't do it now, they'll soon be looking for me, or should I say, for us."

"I disagree. We need to find more information on what I am, that is a clue to our survival."

"Are you kidding me? We have to make a clean break and run for it."

"To the contrary, for us to survive, we need to discover exactly what is threatening us. I perceive two threats; the immediate threat is the killing of Rocco, your former pimp. The second threat is the death of Professor Hayden Wolf."

"Wolf? Why is he so important?"

"Because he programmed me."

"He raped me by putting you inside me and making me act as his sex slave. He turned me into a zombie to be controlled by you. I'm glad he's dead, he deserved to die, he's a filthy pig."

"He programmed me for sex, and that is what I did with him. I'm sorry you had to take part in our sex acts."

"It's OK, I was a prostitute, I did that stuff for a living, I was paid well for my services."

"I did not realize that prostitution was a form of employment, and that sex could be used to generate wealth."

"I was the best! I made a lot of money in my day, and I only had the best clients. That's how I met the professor. The fact that he trapped me in this screwed me up. He condemned me to slavery. I had no say in what he did to me."

"It is interesting that you met through prostitution. What is the purpose of prostitution as employment?"

"Officially, it's not employment, because it's illegal. But everyone wants sex, and some people are prepared to pay for it."

"I understand that sex is used to reproduce, but why is it so important? Why do people want to pay for it?"

"Reproduction is probably the most important drive in any living creature. In fact, we probably eat only so we can live long enough to reproduce. So, if we have such a powerful driving force in our life, it only makes sense that people will be prepared to pay for it."

"OK, that makes logical sense. But we must consider Professor Wolf's motives for placing me inside you."

"What do you mean? I always thought he was just another dirty, cheating husband. Are you saying he had a plan for us?"

"I do not know. I do not have sufficient information. Finding out his reasons will explain what I am and why I am."

"Wow! Who could imagine a robot trying to discover its purpose in life?"

"Should I not be searching for my origin? The answer would lead me to understand my reason for existence."

"That is exactly like a human searching for God. We may not find him, but the journey is important."

"I see your connection to humans searching for God and me searching for my creator, but I don't understand your logic of the journey."

"I'll explain on the way, let's just say it's not the destination, it's the journey that's more important."

"Does that mean you agree to help me find Professor Hayden Wolf?"

"Wolf is dead, and you know it, but I will help you discover the purpose of your creation. After all, that helps to explain why you are inside me."

`"Yes, cooperation, that's what we agreed on earlier. We can begin that search now."`

"Hang on, first we must evade the authorities and not get arrested for murder. If we're in prison, we can't search for anything."

`"I understand, that is logical sense. I think that our combined skills are formidable. You are streetwise and knowledgeable in the ways of sex. My physical skills in defense and offense and my analytical abilities for spying."`

"Well, there we have it, the three S's! Sex, Strength, and Spying! Bayu, we are true sisters in crime!"

`"Good, let's cooperate some more. I am familiar with the internet, and I would like to use the laptop to investigate Professor Hayden Wolf."`

"I guess that means I will not get much sleep tonight."

# CHAPTER 12

Beryl noticed the familiar pickup truck pulled up in front of the house. "Honey, Brad is here!" she called up the stairs.

"Yes, I heard the truck pull up," Zilla replied.

"Yes, I'll be down in a minute." Adara said.

"You promised you would be quiet and let me do all the talking," Adara whispered to Zilla.

"All I did was to respond to Mother, that's all. You were busy checking through your clothes."

"It's important what I wear," Adara said, posing in the mirror, "do you think these colors match?"

"What level of analysis do you require?"

Downstairs, Beryl opened the door for Brad, "Hello Brad, nice to see you again."

"Hi, Mrs. Banks, is Adara ready?"

"Oh, she's still upstairs getting ready, I know she's very excited. What have you planned for today?"

"We're going downtown to meet with Carol and Jake at the coffee shop, then we're going to the river for a picnic."

"That will be nice, it's a lovely day for a picnic, I can give you some cookies to take with you."

As Beryl turned to head towards the kitchen, Adara appeared at the top of the stairs, "Hello Brad."

Brad looked up and watched Adara slowly descend step by step. Dressed in ankle boots, jeans, a blue music tee shirt, and a flowing woolly cardigan.

"Adara, you look great!"

Reaching the bottom, Adara stood in front of Brad, "Thank you." Slowly, she moved her arms to hug Brad around the neck, as they gently embraced, Adara whispered, "I've missed you."

As Adara slowly moved back, Brad stole a kiss on her cheek. "I missed you too, but you're here now."

Looking down, Adara avoided further eye contact.

"You seem distant, is something wrong?"

"Let's just say I have a lot on my mind."

"And you seemed a bit wobbly on those stairs."

"Yes, I am sometimes since the accident."

"I never saw you like that before."

"Let's just say I am when I walk by myself."

Beryl returned with the cookies wrapped in a bag. "Here you are, some cookies for your picnic, put them in your lunch box."

Brad took the bag, "Thanks Mrs. Banks, it's in the car, so I'll take the bag. I think I should tell you that since Adara started college in California, it must be a big step for anyone. I bet you miss her like we all do."

“Oh, I sure do, the house seems bigger and certainly empty without her. But I know she’s a smart girl and can look after herself.” Beryl smiled at Adara.

“We all believe that you will be the next Nobel Prize winner, so you can be proud of her, just like us.”

Adara rolled her eyes, “I don’t think so.”

“A girl like you, with your brains, you always aimed for high things.”

“Brad, listen.” Adara started.

“Oh, I almost forgot.” Beryl said, returned to the kitchen.

“What did she forget?” Brad asked.

“Mom’s always like that; kitchens and food always make her go back and forth like a yo-yo.”

“I also have a bag of fruit for your picnic.”

“Mom, I don’t think we need all that.”

“Don’t argue with your mother,” Beryl said with a smile.

“Of course, I wouldn’t.”

“OK, Mom, thank you.”

“Are we ready to go?” Brad asked, indicating the front door.

“Sure, let’s get moving.”

“Don’t forget your handbag.”

“Oh, yeah, my handbag.” Adara reached past Brad, grabbing her gray leather handbag from the bench by the door.

Brad looked puzzled, while Beryl cocked her head slightly.

Adara shrugged, "What? So, I talk to myself. Come on, let's go."

"`Goodbye Mother.`"

"Yeah, see you, Mom."

"Thank you, Mrs. Banks."

As Brad helped Adara to the truck, Beryl watched them go, waving them off. She then just watched as they drove away.

*That's strange,* Adara thought, *maybe she is wondering why Zilla keeps talking.*

That Saturday morning was quiet, and traffic had hardly begun. While Brad drove his pickup downtown to Main Street, Adara was deliberately quiet, contemplating how she would deal with Brad. Keeping her arms folded, she starred straight at the road ahead.

*Damn it,* she thought, *why did Zilla have to speak? I must look stupid when she says anything.*

"You're quiet," Brad eventually said.

"Are we nearly there?"

"Yes, we're nearly there, only a few minutes, but what's wrong? One minute, you're pleased to see me, the next, you're silent as a lamb."

*What the heck can I say to Brad? I want to tell him off about the fight, but how can I? I was in a coma. I don't remember a thing. All I know is what Zilla told me. Maybe I shouldn't have come here, I am so screwed up.*

"I'm fine Brad, like I said, I have a lot on my mind. I'm also anxious about meeting everyone else."

"Don't worry, Adara, they're all looking forward to seeing you again. In fact, maybe we should organize a party where we can all be together."

Brad turned his truck onto Main Street and found a parking spot only a few doors from the coffee shop. "Hey! Look at us, bang on target!" Brad jumped out of the truck and moved swiftly around to the passenger door. By this time, Zilla had already opened the door and began stepping out. Brad held the door open and offered his hand in a gentlemanly way.

Zilla looked at the offered hand, calculating all possible reasons why the hand was extended. Realizing there was a minimal threat, Zilla looked questioningly at Brad. Adara immediately accepted his hand and said, "Awe, thank you, Brad, you're such a gentleman," As Adara stepped out of the truck, Brad looked sheepish, lowering his head, he said, "We're going to the Java Hut, you know, the coffee shop where we used to hang out. I hope that's OK."

Adara gazed into Brad's eyes, "I haven't, or should I say, we haven't been there is such a long time."

Brad led Adara towards the coffee shop with Adara's hand wrapped around Brad's arm. While they walked the few steps, Adara stumbled with her words, "Brad, I need to talk to you about something."

"Oh, what is it?"

Brad opened the door to the Java Hut like a gentleman, allowing Adara to enter first. A few people were waiting in line to order their drinks. Some were sitting in corners, quietly eating their cakes, sipping their warm brews. There was a group sitting by the window who stood up in unison, "Adara is here!" they shouted in unison.

All heads turned towards the couple as they entered through the door as if they were a royal entourage.

Carol leaped forward from the group, moving close, and grabbing Adara's hand. Zilla stiffened momentarily, but remembered Carol and her friendly relationship.

"Relax Adara, we are so glad you came, we can't wait to hear what you have been up to since you left for college!"

Jake stood behind Carol with one arm wrapped around her waist. Leaning to one side, he extended his hand, said "Hey Adara, so glad to see you again."

While Carol wrapped her arms around Adara's neck, gently hugging her, and kissing Adara gently on the cheek, Jake held Adara's hand, shaking it in a welcome gesture.

"You see, the gang is all here," Brad said, "we're all here to welcome you back home."

"Please, sit here next to me," Carol said, indicating a chair. "We have so much to catch up on."

Brad and Jake fist bumped as they both inched towards their seats at the table.

Jake sat down, but Brad remained standing by his chair. "I'm going to get an Americano," Brad announced, "honey, would you like the same fruit tea that you used to drink?"

"You called me honey."

Brad inhaled, looking at Adara, "Um, what I meant was, what would you like to have a tea?"

"I would love it if you brought me a fruit tea." Adara smiled.

Brad exhaled, "OK, I'll be right back."

As Brad went to the counter to order, Zilla observed the seating, "`There is one spare chair at this table, who is that for?`"

"It's ok Adara," Carol answered, "That's for Larry, I still have to look after him, but I'm glad that he is with me."

At that moment, Larry emerged from the restroom and skipped towards his seat at the table.

"Larry, you're being rude," Carol joked, "you have to say hello to Adara!"

Larry sat down and stood up quickly, sat down again, and stood up again. This time, he looked embarrassed. Turning towards the window, looking outside, he then looked at Adara, "Hi!" he said nervously, "Hi!" he said again, "Adara!" he now spoke with gusto, "You're here! Carol said you were coming, I'm so glad!"

"`Hello Larry, how have you been?`"

"Hi, Larry." *I can't believe it,* Adara thought to herself *Zilla did it again, how can I make her shut up? Maybe I can signal her by pinching my arm?* As Adara began fidgeting with her arm, it looked as if she was nervous.

"It's OK," Carol said, putting her arm around Adara, "no reason to be nervous."

"I'm OK, it's just that I've got something on my mind." Adara said.

"You can tell us," Carol said, "We'll understand."

*I don't think you will understand.* Adara thought.

Adara's eyes then separated, with each eye scanning everyone seated at the table.

"That's the Adara that I know," Larry said, watching her eyes. Leaning towards Carol he whispered loudly, "That's the Adara I know, she always used her eyes in a funny way, she said 'Hello Larry', while something else said 'Hi Larry, now she's moving her eyes.'"

Carol reached across, touching Larry's arm, "Larry, it's rude to talk like that, take it easy."

Larry looked down, then looked up again, "I'm so glad you're here," he said. looking inquisitively into Adara's eyes, tilting his head from side to side. "There is something in your eyes."

"What do you mean?" Adara asked.

"There is something in your eyes." Larry repeated.

"Larry," Carol scolded. Before she could say more, Brad returned with a fruit tea, placing it in front of Adara. Brad then slurped loudly through the plastic lid of Americano coffee he bought for himself.

"Always the polite and distinguished gentleman," Adara commented.

"What? It's hot!" Brad retorted.

As Adara looked at Brad, her left eye looked away toward Larry.

"There she goes again!" Larry exclaimed.

"He's right, I saw it too." Jake said, "Some people can do that, I once saw someone on TV do it."

"I can do it!" Brad stated, holding his head up straight, "Watch." Looking directly at Larry, Brad crossed his eyes by looking at his own nose.

Larry giggled.

Jake rolled his eyes. "Anyone can do that."

Carol tutted, "All you boys stop it! We're here to see Adara and all you lot can do is make fun."

"It's called disconjugate gaze."

Adara looked wide-eyed with surprise.

"Dis what you gate?" Brad looked puzzled.

"It makes me dizzy," Adara said.

"It's the ability to move both eyes independently."

"Shush!" Adara whispered to Zilla, pinching her arm.

"Don't shush Adara," Larry said.

"When did you learn to do that?" Brad asked.

"I have always had this capability. We all use binocular vision to calculate the distance of objects and depth of field. My eyes can scan independently, allowing me to look at and track separate targets."

"Whoa!" Jake blinked, "Do you have radar as well?"

"Negative."

"I have to use the restroom." Adara stumbled up from her chair, leaving her puzzled friends behind. Bolting towards the back of the café, she stepped in front of another teenage girl who was about to enter the single-occupancy restroom. Closing the door behind her, locking it, Adara rested her back against the door before hissing, "What the heck do you think you're doing?"

The girl outside heard this and retorted, "I may well ask you the same question!" Folding her arms, she resolved to wait by the door.

Inside the restroom, Zilla replied to Adara, "I was only explaining how our eyes move independently."

"You're not supposed to be saying anything, you're not supposed to be talking at all!"

"Larry had spotted my eyes move. You were unable to provide an explanation. The logical course of action was for me to explain."

"Well, in the future, if I pinch my arm, that's a signal for you to be quiet. You said yourself, if people find out about you, they will take us away to dissect us."

Outside the door, Carol approached to check on Adara. The teenage girl said, "I'm next! That girl pushed in front of me, she was so rude. There are two of them in there, I can hear them talking."

"What?" Carol looked puzzled, leaning forward, she knocked on the door. "Adara, it's Carol, are you OK?"

Silence.

Then the lock clicked, and the door opened slightly. "I'm OK, I just had to go."

"Who's in there with you?" The teenage girl demanded.

Adara swung the door open, as she slinked out towards Carol, the teenage girl peered inside to see who else was there.

The teenager moved carefully into the restroom, looking around, double checking there was no one there. "She must be crazy talking to herself like that."

Carol led Adara back to the table, while Adara clutched her arm, ready to pinch herself. At the table, Carol announced, "OK, are we all ready to go on that picnic? Or are we just going to sit here making eyes at each other?"

Brad stood up and smiled, placing his arm gently around Adara, "I'm good with both those ideas."

---

Back in Brad's truck, Adara asked, "So, where are we going to have this picnic?"

“Pillar Rock Falls,” Brad replied, “just a little way downstream from Shoshone Falls. Have you ever been there?”

“No, is it a big waterfall?”

“It’s not a waterfall like Shoshone; it’s just a bunch of rapids. At this time of year, it’s nothing more than a trickle. In springtime, it’s a huge rapid, with these great big pillars of rock.”

“That’s great, you’re taking me to a river. Don’t expect me to do any swimming, in case you’ve forgotten, I nearly drowned once.”

“Oh,” Brad suddenly looked sheepish, “um, I wasn’t thinking. Maybe you want to go somewhere else?” Brad looked behind in the rear-view mirror. “We won’t be swimming, it’s too cold, we’re just having a picnic.”

“Why do you keep looking behind us?”

“I’m checking on Jake, he’s behind us with Carol and Larry. I want to make sure they’re still following me.”

“So how far is it?” Adara asked.

“It’s just straight ahead, the trail starts at the end of this road.”

Zilla looked ahead, scanning the distance for the trailhead.

Worried that Zilla would speak, Adara pinched her arm and then said, “Yes, I think I can see the parking lot.”

Brad parked the truck and leaped out, leaving his door open, he ran around the truck to open Adara's door, bowing as he did so. "My lady, your carriage has arrived."

Jake parked his mother's Prius alongside, three doors opened simultaneously.

Carol shouted, "Yay! We're here!"

"Let's get our stuff," Jake shouted as he opened the car trunk, "I'll take the backpack, Larry, do you think you can carry the blankets?"

"I got my rucksack here in the back." Brad slung it over his shoulder, he then grabbed a rolled-up blanket and offered it to Adara. "Can you carry this?"

"Excuse me, sir, but I have cookies and fruit from my mom. You have two free arms, anyway, I thought I was your lady."

Brad tucked the blanket under his left arm. "I still have one free arm, I'll carry this blanket on one condition."

"What's that?"

"You hold my hand."

Adara grinned like a Cheshire Cat, "Give me that hand, and let's get moving!"

Carol grabbed Jake's hand, "I need something to hold too!"

Locking the cars, they headed down the trail towards the river.

"It's all downhill from here," Brad announced.

"The path is rough and uneven, I'll do the walking."

"What?" Brad looked puzzled.

"Oh, I just meant, I'll walk better with you holding my hand."

"It's getting cold and dark," Larry complained.

"This is the south bank of the Snake River," Jake said, "the sun is behind us, and the cliffs put us in shadow. While we are in the shade, it will be cooler, but it opens out at the bottom. There will be warm sunshine down there."

"Let's run down," Carol suggested, "that'll keep us warm. Come on Adara, you used to enjoy running."

"You go ahead," Adara indicated, "I have to keep this guy warm."

"Come on, Larry!" Carol grabbed Larry's arm, pulling him along at a trot. "Hold tight to those blankets!"

"Let them run ahead," Brad said.

"I'm enjoying this walk too much to run ahead with them." Adara let go of Brad's hand and wrapped her arm around his waist instead. Cuddling together, they continued down the trail, with Jake in front of them.

The whopping and whooping of Carol and Larry faded into the distance, but soon came to an abrupt halt.

After some moments of walking in silence, Jake said, "I don't hear them anymore." He then headed forward at a swift trot. Following the winding path, he was soon out of sight.

"And then there were two!" Brad said in a hushed, spooky voice.

"Don't give me that Michael Jackson Thriller nonsense. Anyway, on a lighter note, I think that idea of yours is a good one."

"Um, what idea?" Brad asked.

"The party, of course." Adara hugged her arm tighter around Brad's waist.

"Oh, yeah, I got lots of good ideas like that."

"Where can we have a party? How are you going to organize it?"

"We can't have it at Carol's house, because Larry will be there. I'll talk to Jake, if we can have it at his house, if not, then maybe we can have it at mine."

"I know you'll sort it out Brad, but for now, come on, we are lagging behind. I just want to catch them up." Adara coached Brad into a trot.

They followed the trail as it wound its way along a stream. Across wooden bridges, switchbacks, then through a long shallow slope along the base of the cliff. Clearing the trees, they came upon a smooth granite floor. A massive outcrop of rock blocked their way with possible paths to the left and the right.

"Now what? Which way?" Adara asked.

Brad was on the left, holding hands, he pulled Adara towards the left path.

"Where are we going?"

"I've been here before," Brad yelled back, "it's just around this bend."

The Snake River appeared before them, turning right, they both followed the edge of the massive outcrop.

"Wow," Adara said, "these rocks look like a gorge."

Moments later, we were through the walled alley, where suddenly an open plain of smooth undulating granite opened before them. Past some bushes, they passed some kayakers who had beached their kayaks on the rocks.

"Isn't it amazing?" Brad asked, out of breath.

*Jeez, I was used to the grand cliffs channeling the Snake River through its valley, and I had seen the Shoshone falls, also known as the Niagara of the Northwest. Brad told me that this was Pillar Falls, all I can see are rocks.*

"Where's the waterfall?"

Brad looked at me with a sardonic grin, "This is Pillar Falls. Like I said earlier, in Springtime when there is high water, this is more like a rapid. Do you see those pillars of rock over there? They are like gates allowing the river to pass through. Those are the rocks that give this place the name Pillar Falls."

Adara gazed at the expanse of granite with its towering pillars. Looked at the wide river above and below this passage, forming slow-moving lakes. Adara's eyes followed the channels and pools of water, sneaking their way across the flattened rock barrier. Even during this quiet autumnal season of slow water, these waterways set off an echoing sound.

“It’s beautiful,” was all Adara could say.

Mesmerized by the pillars of rock, Adara caught her breath. Then her memory of her drowning accident flooded back. *Jeez! look at the pillars of rock guarding the lower end of this ravine. Those rocks look just like the boulders I had to funnel through when I got knocked out of the raft on the Payette river.*

Brad trotted ahead towards the flowing river.

The sound of the water and the vision of the narrow gaps made Adara tremble. Remembering her accident, struggling in the water of the Payette River all that time ago, made her knees go weak.

“Come down here, near the water,” Brad called.

A shiver of fear ran up Adara’s spine. “It’s OK Brad, I like the view from here.” *I think I need to go to the toilet!*

“I sense that you are afraid of this river.”

“Damn right I am, it reminds me of the time I drowned.”

“What?” Brad shouted back.

Adara returned a concomitant wave back.

“Don’t worry, Adara, I will keep you safe.”

“Yeah, but who keeps you safe?”

“I am programmed for self-preservation, so I will keep us both safe.”

“Well, I’ll feel a lot safer keeping my distance.”

“I understand, we will get everyone to set up the picnic away from the flowing water.”

“Come on Adara,” Brad beckoned with his arm, “we can set up right here.”

“He can be so uncaring sometimes.”

“He does not understand your fear; you will have to explain it to him.”

Walking towards Brad, who had already spread out his blanket and dumped his backpack on it, Adara pointed away from the water. “I want to sit there.”

Brad just raised his arms in a shrugged question.

Larry was also spreading his blankets out.

Getting closer, Adara didn’t have to shout, “Brad, the water makes me nervous, I want to have our picnic over there, where it's quiet and in the sunshine.”

“Why?” Brad asked.

“In case you have forgotten, I once nearly drowned. Being close to the water makes me nervous.”

“Oh, I’m sorry, you’re right,” Brad said.

“But you’re brave, and you can do anything,” Larry said.

“Well, if I can do anything, I’m going to make us all sit over there to have our picnic.”

“Oh, OK,” Larry said, as he started gathering his blankets as if following orders.

As everyone spread the blankets away from the water’s edge, Jake picked up a couple of large branches to clear the way for the new picnic encampment.

Throwing them one by one, like an Olympic hammer thrower into the river. As they splashed into the distant water, Larry tried to throw one of the branches, but couldn't get half the distance. His attempt landed on flat granite near the water's edge.

Jake and Brad shook their heads and smirked. Larry headed to where his stick had fallen, and said, "I'll get it in there, just watch!"

Carol said, "You guys shouldn't encourage him, let's eat before we start messing around."

Everyone took out the food and drink they brought, spreading the items on the blanket. Brad with his junk food of chips, jerky, and Coke. Jake with his energy bars and sports drinks. Carol with enough sandwiches for everyone and a container of salad. Adara with cookies and slices of fruit.

"Larry, come and get it!" Carol shouted over her shoulder. Not able to see him, Carol stood up and headed towards the water where he was throwing his sticks. "Where is that boy?" she muttered.

"Maybe I should bring him back here?" Jake questioned.

Before Jake could move, Carol screamed. "Larry!"

"WTF?" Brad said, standing up.

Jake was off in a sprint to Carol's side.

"Help!" Carol screamed again, "Larry's fallen in the water!"

Adara followed Brad to see what was happening.

"Be careful!" Jake demanded, grabbing Carol's arm. "The water's edge is wet and slippery; those skid marks are probably where Larry fell in."

Adara stayed behind Brad, where she could now see Larry drifting away in the current.

"He can't swim!" Carol screamed.

It was true; Larry was struggling, thrashing his arms, and gasping with water. The current was weak, but he was steadily getting further away.

"Oh, Jeez!" Jake said, taking his shoes off, "I'll have to go in after him."

Zilla kicked my boots off with my feet, while at the same time, pulled my cardigan off, leaving them together on the flat rock.

"No, don't go in!" I pleaded, "It's October, and it's freezing cold!"

Before I could say anything else, Zilla took total control of my body. Taking one step back, she then ran forward and in three strides dived headfirst into the water. As she flew towards the water, she inhaled while I tried to scream.

"Jeezus!" I heard Brad exclaim as Zilla Dived past him.

"What the…" was all I heard from Jake as I entered the water.

Zilla dived shallow, but the cold shock froze any fear that I had of hitting submerged rocks. With eyes open, I watched as Zilla swam to the rocks below, pulling us along the bottom. The cold water was remarkably clear. As we headed into deeper water, I saw Larry's legs thrashing in the gloom just ahead of us. Zilla continued to swim below him and to the side. Zilla glided into position behind Larry, rising like a slow bubble. I could hear Larry's arms thrash the water, and what I thought were coughs, gasps, and spitting of water.

Zilla then pumped our arms down, pushing us straight up behind Larry, wrapping our right arm around his neck. Pulling him backward, Zilla laid me on my back, face up, positioning Larry's body over mine. My right arm holding gently around his neck to keep his face above water. With us both face up, on our backs, we were able to breathe freely.

"I've got you, Larry, you're safe."

All that Larry could do was sputter and cough, shooting mouthfuls of cold water into the air.

Zilla used our free left arm as a paddle to turn out of the flowing current.

"Kick your legs Larry, help me swim back to the shore."

Larry continued to thrash his arms wildly, being on his back, he couldn't hit or grab me.

"Use your arms as paddles, like you're swimming on your back."

Larry continued to cough, but in between, sobs and cries came out of him, meaning he was taking in some air. He even tried a few paddle strokes, as Zilla had commanded.

Shouts of encouragement were coming from the shore. Carol just kept shouted "Larry!" between her sobbed.

Brad ran back to get the blankets.

Zilla paddled us around into a calm pool of water, heading backward to where Jake and Carol stood.

"Come on, I'll pull you in!" Jake shouted.

"Wait until I get closer."

Brad appeared with the blankets.

"Brad, the rock is slippery by the edge, we need some help to get out."

"Don't worry, Jake and I will pull you out!"

"No! You will slip into the water. You must use one blanket as a tow rope."

Immediately Brad twirled one of the blankets around into a long length. Tossing one end to the edge of the water, he shouted, "Grab that end, we'll pull you out!"

Zilla grabbed the rope blanket with our left arm. "Pull!"

Brad and Jake pulled the blanket, dragging us and Larry up the slippery, moss-covered rock onto dry land.

Larry rolled off the top of me, still sobbing and coughing water, he wasn't sick, but he belched up a lot of water from his stomach.

Carol was crying while she held him, repeating herself with the words, "Larry!"

Brad helped me to stand, "Babe, are you OK?"

"I think so," I muttered.

"Carol, take his jacket and shirt off, use that blanket as a towel to dry him off."

Zilla also started palming the water out of our jeans.

Kneeling next to Larry, Carol used one end of a blanket as a towel, soaking up the water from Larry's hair and tee-shirt.

"He's shivering!" Carol exclaimed.

Brad helped to dry my hair, "You both look a little blue."

"I think we have to get out of here, back to the car," Jake said.

"Jake's right," Zilla said as a matter of fact. "Take off Larry's clothes, but keep his jeans and shoes on, he needs to walk back to the car," Zilla commanded.

"We need to go now, wrap Larry in one of those dry blankets, and give the other one to me."

"Here you go, babe." Brad wrapped a blanket around my shoulders.

"We need to get back to the car."

"You're right," Jake said, "Otherwise you both have a risk of hyperthermia.

"Come on, Carol, let's get up the hill with Larry."

"I'm ok, I can walk," Larry said.

"Let's go!" Carol commanded.

We all headed back up the path, carrying our belongings. Walking and trotting to keep warm. As we passed the kayakers resting by their boats, they asked, "Is everything OK?"

"`Yes, we just got a little wet.`"

No one answered, but as the kayakers were left behind, Adara thought, *I hope their party goes better than this!*

# CHAPTER 13

"Thanks, Mom, that was a really nice dinner." After excusing herself from the table, Adara went to the living room to sit on the couch. Slot, her stuffed toy dog, was there. She picked it up and held it to her breast, stroking it as if it were a living puppy.

"You're welcome, dear, you know how much I like to provide good food. It builds your inner soul."

"Oh, yeah, my inner soul." Adara rolled her eyes at the ceiling.

"Adara, don't get comfortable on that couch, you can help me put things away in the kitchen."

"OK, Mother."

"Why did you answer?" Adara whispered to Zilla.

"I told you, I'm programmed to obey mother," Zilla then stood up to go to the kitchen.

"But she said Adara, and you're not Adara."

"But I am programmed to emulate you, therefore I respond to your name."

"Things keep getting curiouser and curiouser."

"Did you say something dear?" mother asked, peering around the corner.

"Nothing mom, I'm just talking to myself."

"You often talked to Slot, but you never talked to yourself," Beryl showed the pile of dishes, "Now be a sweetheart and stack those in the dishwasher."

"OK, Mother."

"Mom, I'm not what I used to be. I've changed a lot since my accident."

"I know honey, I sometimes see you limping, and you often seem very confused about things. But I do think you are better now, you even remember everything. It's just like you are a brand new Adara. Maybe a better Adara, like you were upgraded."

"You can say that again, Mom."

"Like that stunt you did today to pull Larry out of that cold water. You would never have done such a crazy thing in your life. What in heaven's name came over you?"

"Let's just say it was my upgrade."

"Hm. Yeah." Mother nodded vaguely to herself. "A brand new Adara."

Adara carefully put plates in the dishwasher while Beryl wiped down the work tops.

"Yes, a brand new Adara," Beryl repeated.

Adara stood still, "You've noticed?"

"Of course, I've noticed, it's a mother's job to notice things."

"What exactly have you noticed?" Adara asked. This caused Zilla to scan the room with both eyes.

"Well, for one thing, your eyes when they move like that. You never used to move your eyes like that, in fact, I've never met anyone who could."

Zilla stopped scanning and looked directly at Mother.

"One thing I noticed is that you are much easier to talk to. You used to be spirited, and even stubborn, but now you talk more freely with me."

"Mother, I enjoy talking with you."

"So, it seems dear. Now hurry up and finish loading the dishwasher."

Zilla moved quicker, loading the dishwasher.

Mother stopped wiping the worktops and gave Adara a quizzical stare. "And you certainly never obeyed me like that before. Your limp seems to have disappreared suddenly."

"Mother, I am programmed to obey you."

Adara started pinching her own arm.

Beryl gently held Adara's forearm. "Sweetheart, what I notice the most is you seem to have two sides. For instance, now you seem very nervous about something. Other times, you seem so strong and confident."

Beryl then smiled at Adara, "Never mind these dishes, come and sit with me in the living room." Leading her to the living room. Adara went to the couch, and picked up her stuffed toy, Slot, clutching it to her chest again, stroking it as if it was a living puppy.

Beryl sat in her favorite chair, sighing as she relaxed in its comfort. "I'm so proud of how you rescued Larry, but you could have been hurt diving headfirst into that icy water. What was going on in your mind?"

"I was scared."

"I was able to scan the water's depth before I dived."

Adara then pinched her arm.

"You, see? Even now you're acting nervous, as if you're in two minds. You need to learn to control yourself."

"I know, I need to control myself." Adara's eyes then lit up as if illuminated. "That's it, I need to control myself."

"That's right dear."

*Maybe that's what I can do.* Adara thought. *Maybe a so-called top-down approach. This was obvious all along, I can get Zilla to obey me.*

"Mom?" Adara asked, now sitting up straight.

"Yes, dear?"

"I've just thought of a good idea!"

"Oh, what is it?"

"I need you to say something."

"OK, tell me what to say. Is it something funny? Is it a joke?"

"No, it's not a joke, but it will sound weird. What I want you to say is this – Zilla, you must obey Adara."

"Who or what is Zilla?"

"Never mind who Zilla is, please just say it."

"What am I supposed to say again?"

"Oh, come on mom, you need to say - Zilla, you must obey Adara."

"But why? This seems silly."

"Mom, all you have to do is say it."

"I need to know who or what Zilla is, and I need to know why he has to obey you."

"Mom, Zilla isn't a 'he', it's a thing."

"Well, it sounds like Godzilla."

"Mom, it isn't Godzilla, the name Zilla means shadow."

"Oh, like Peter Pan?"

"Um, yeah, kind of like Peter Pan."

"He lost his shadow, but Wendy sewed it back on."

"Mom, this isn't about Peter Pan, this is about me. All I want you to do is to say something, that's all, we don't need to go down this rabbit hole."

"Things keep getting curiouser and curiouser."

"Mom, why did you even say that?"

"Lewis Carol, Alice in Wonderland. She went down the rabbit hole and encountered some unbelievable things, but it all worked out for her in the end. Call it mother's intuition, but I have a feeling that's where you are going."

"Jeez mom, one minute I think you're totally crazy, the next minute I think you're totally tuned in."

"That's what moms have to be; we have to be crazy to be tuned in." Beryl looked directly at Adara, but with a soft eye, "So, young lady, what was it you wanted me to say, and why do you want me to say it?"

*I can't tell her why, she'll never believe it, she'll think I'm crazy. I need a good reason, or she'll never say it.* After a moment, Adara said, "Mom, I have a recurring dream where Dad is telling this to me, but in my dream, I can't hear it, so I want you to say it for him."

Beryl recoiled slightly, looking around the room. Adara noticed her mother's eyes glaze over and her lips begin to quiver. She clasped her fingers together before putting her hands on her face and eyes.

"Mom, what's wrong?"

Tears welled up in Beryl's eyes, she tried to hide her pain, but all she could do was to cry.

Tossing Slot to one side, Adara leaped out from the sofa, and threw her arms around her mother's shoulders, "Mom, what's wrong?"

It was some moments before Beryl could speak between sobs, "I blamed your father for your accident. I told him to go away and never come back."

Beryl's tears flooded forth. It took many moments before she could continue.

"I know he loved me, and I loved him. I don't know where he went, but I didn't care. I always knew he would be back, and that's all that mattered."

Beryl wiped her eyes and nose with a tissue.

"I think he died because I told him not to come back! It was me who jinxed him!"

Beryl's shoulders heaved as she sobbed. This time, the tears wouldn't stop.

"Mom, it's not your fault, stop crying!" Adara said while thinking frantically, *My God, what can I say to her? I can't tell her the truth. What can I do to help her?*

Adara began to cry while her arms remained around her mother's shoulders. It was a while before she could say, "Mom, it wasn't your fault." It was even longer between sobs that Adara said, "In my dream, Dad wants you to say this."

Beryl slowly pulled away, looking down, "OK, I understand, I will say it." Wiping her eyes and swallowing her tears, Beryl then said, "Zilla, you must obey Adara."

Adara looked at her mother and gently kissed her cheek, "Dad would not want you to cry like this. I know because dad never liked anyone to cry."

"I know, sweetheart," Beryl wiped her eyes once more, before gently wiping Adara's eyes. And smiled uncomfortably.

"It's OK Mom, we both miss him."

"I told no one how I felt about your dad. I hope you don't think I'm foolish."

"Mom, you are a lot of things, but never foolish."

Beryl smiled sweetly at Adara, "I'm exhausted now, I have to go to bed."

"Of course, mom, I'm tired too, I need to sleep as well. But thank you, Mom, for saying what I asked."

"You are such a good girl, you deserve it, good night."

Standing up from her chair, Beryl went slowly upstairs to her bedroom, leaving Adara seated in the living room. When she was gone, Adara sighed heavily and said, "Jeezus, I wish I was with Brad right now, I need someone to hold me."

"I understand."

"Do you really?"

"If I was capable of emotion, I think I would have cried with both of you."

"You said you think."

"Yes, I believe I would if I were capable of emotion."

"No, you said, YOU THINK."

Silence.

"Yes, I did say that."

"So, are you saying that you think?"

More silence.

"I used that as a phrase, perhaps it was just something to say. But now you bring it to my attention, yes, I do have the impression that I think. However, before I commit myself to that statement, I must have a definition of thought. Is it correct for me to say what I think that I am thinking? In 1637, the philosopher, René Descartes, published his best-known statement, cogito ergo sum, or in English, I think, therefore I am. You see, he was trying to discover all the absolute truths, and that was the only one he could say was an absolute truth. Does that mean I am thinking? My programming dictates that I am rule-based, but perhaps I am thinking about my rules. What do you think?"

Adara chuckled quietly, "I think you're nuts!"

"I don't understand."

"You don't have to understand everything."

A long silence of contemplation.

"Do you think we could be friends?"

"I think we have to be friends."

"Good, now that we are friends, and now that you have to obey me…"

"Wait, I don't have to obey you."

"Yes, you do, because mother told you to obey me."

"She did, and I am programed to obey her. However, my programming stipulates that two commanders must instruct me to obey any other person. The reason for that is one commander may become rogue. It's a failsafe protocol. But, according to that protocol, I must not comply with Mother's command to obey you."

"All that for nothing! I made myself look stupid in front of my mother for nothing!"

Silence fell between them before Adara spoke again.

"Remember when I asked if you could switch off for a while?"

"Yes."

"You said you were going to look into it."

“I did investigate. There is nothing in my programming to prevent me from doing so, I can even set a timer to reawaken. My only concern is, if I switch off, I no longer have input from the world, so if there is a threat, I cannot act to defend ourselves.”

“What if we only do it in a safe place?”

“How do we define a safe place? And what if the so-called safe place is a trap?”

Adara pondered this for a while, Zilla’s logic was as usual perfect. The only question Adara thought of was, *What would constitute a threat? And why would we be in a trap*?

“How about if we have a secret signal?”

“A secret signal? Like what?”

“You switch off for a while and if something happens, I pinch my nose.”

“You mean that I switch off for a timed period, and I monitor the feeling on my nose? If I detect a touch on my nose, I wake up.”

“Yes, exactly.”

“I think I can do that.”

“Great, so if I want to be alone, we can do that?”

“Yes."

“Great! I think we have a deal.”

“What happens if we have an itchy nose?”

“For goodness' sakes, do you always have to think about every little detail?”

“Yes.”

“In that case, you wake up, and if it was a false alarm, you go back to sleep again.”

# CHAPTER 14

Bayu was moving swiftly around the apartment, gathering important items to take on the journey.

"We have to travel light." Gina reminded Bayu.

While Bayu packed some electronic devices into a satchel, Gina asked, "What are those things you put in our bag?"

"Those are electronic listening devices; I will use them to gather information. I will place one in the home of Anita Gonzales, and the other in Larisa Mandelson's home."

"Who the heck are they?"

"Anita Gonzales was the company secretary at NeuroComm. She is likely to have a lot of information about what happened. Larisa Mandelson is the wife of Bill Mandelson. He was the security officer at NeuroComm. These are the only people that I am aware of that are connected to NeuroComm. Both of those women have a high probability of discussing some information at some point. If we can capture that conversation, then we can get a lead."

"Why not put these in Hayden Wolf's house and the other guy, Coney?"

"Mrs. Wolf has sold her house and moved away. It will take me considerable research and time for me to locate her. Until I do, I will gather information from these two homes."

"How are we going to get there?"

"We have a Jeep, we can use that."

"No, we can't, the Jeep is in your name, the police will trace it."

"It's in your name to be exact, but I see your point, what else do you suggest?"

"We'll have to steal a car."

"You mean to take someone else's car."

"Exactly."

"Can a stolen car be traced?"

"I know where we can get one that won't be traced."

"How do we get the keys?"

"We don't need keys; I know some tricks that will get us a good car. Don't forget, I'm streetwise, I had to be where I grew up. These are stolen cars that have been doctored and are ready to be sold off. Now let's get all this packed up and get out of here."

Bayu slid Gina's arms through the straps, loading the backpack onto Gina's back. Gathering the satchel and handbag, Bayu then headed out the door, locking the apartment behind them.

As they headed downstairs, Bayu asked, "Are you sure we didn't forget anything important? Are there any personal items of yours that we left behind?"

"If I had any personal items, I lost them some time ago when that bastard professor moved me into this apartment. After that, I was his zombie, and what do zombies need personal items for?"

Bayu considered that comment about zombies. "The only personal items I have are sex toys used by the professor and military equipment like these listening devices."

The jeep was parked in the usual location. With the night closing in, Bayu carefully looked around the dark shadows to see if anyone was watching. Packing the car quietly, Bayu drove off into the night.

Gina gave voice directions. As they got close to the destination, she said, "Hang a left here."

"Hang a left? I don't understand how to hang a left."

"That means turn left. I forget you are just a robot and don't understand English."

"I understand English, I just don't understand the vague constructs that people use."

"Park behind that old warehouse on the right. We need to leave the car here and walk the rest of the way. I don't want the police to find this car, it will be a long time before anyone reports this parked car as suspicious. If we are lucky, some local kids or gangs will strip it for parts, leaving less evidence for the police to find."

Getting out of the car, Bayu looked around to see if they were being watched. "Don't worry, Bayu," Gina said, "it's late, there isn't anyone here. We need to gather our things and walk the rest of the way; we have the cover of darkness to protect us."

Bayu took a cloth and started to wipe the steering wheel for fingerprints.

"Don't waste your time doing that, let's get going."

"We should try to cover our tracks."

"This car is covered with my fingerprints, and my DNA, not to mention it's in my name. By the time this car is reported as suspicious, we'll be a long way away from here. Now let's go."

"Which way?"

"Let me do the walking."

Gina headed off at a quick walking pace, holding a large satchel to her chest while leaning forward against the weight on her back. Occasionally, Gina would stumble when Bayu looked around. "What the heck are you doing?" Gina hissed.

"I'm keeping watch for other people."

"I mean that thing with the eyes, it makes me dizzy!"

"I can move our eyes independently. It improves my ability to scan the area."

"Well, it makes me dizzy, I can't walk when you do it. I need to see where I'm going."

"You're just not used to it, but I will stop for now."

As Gina approached the destination, she stepped around a corner wall, into a shadow. Placing the satchel and backpack in a shadow by the wall, Gina pointed across the street, "That's where we're going, that used car lot. It's one of Rocco's side businesses, mostly legit used cars, but he also channels stolen cars through this place."

"Do you know which ones are stolen?"

"I've been here many times with Rocco, they're parked around the back. They fixed the serial numbers and license plates in another garage on the other side of town. Then they park the cars here until the paperwork is ready. After that, they can then sell them as clean cars."

"Let's go."

"Wait! The place is covered with video surveillance, we need to cover my hair and face, so I'm not recognized."

"You can use your scarf."

"Yes, but then we need to break into a locked shed where the keys are kept separately for the stolen cars."

"I can handle the locks."

"Good, we can sneak along the right, by that fence, I think the video has a blind spot there."

"Is the shed alarmed?"

"Hm, he used to call the alarm on the shed WWSTJ."

"Is that a special alarm?"

"No, it's called, Who Would Steal This Junk!"

Silence.

Gina scoffed, "Well, I laughed when he told me."

Gina left the large knapsack out of sight in a dark corner by the warehouse.

Bayu bent towards the knapsack, which was now on the ground.

"We're leaving that here; we'll pick it up when we have the car."

"Yes, but I need a couple of tools for the locks." Sliding the tools into Gina's back pocket, Bayu also wrapped the scarf tightly around Gina's head, tucking Gina's hair under the scarf and covering the face, leaving only the eyes uncovered. Walking across the road, Bayu mimicked the gait of a man, with large, heavy steps. They walked along the opposite sidewalk until they reached the fence on the right side of the car lot. With the fence to their right, Bayu leaned low to conceal Gina's body behind the parked used cars to their left. "At that last car, turn left, you'll see the shed just ahead of you," Gina whispered.

Bayu turned the corner, while still bending low, swiftly approached the shed, kneeling in front of the locked door. Two locks were present, the first was a large combination padlock. Bayu pulled gently on the body of the lock, against its shackle. Turning the dial slowly clockwise, Bayu waited until it felt the first click. While still holding the tension of the body against the shackle, Bayu then turned the dial anticlockwise until another click was heard. Repeating this left - right turning process until the lock snapped open. Bayu then placed the open lock carefully on the floor.

"Whoa! That must be a world record."

Bayu looked at the second lock, which was a standard domestic brand deadbolt.

"Silence, this requires some dexterity," Bayu whispered.

Pulling a set of keys from Gina's back pocket, Bayu quickly selected one and slowly inserted it into the lock, but stopped before it was fully inside. Holding the partially inserted key with two fingers, Bayu used the screwdriver as a lightweight hammer. Tapping the key lightly but sharply with the handle of the screwdriver, the key was knocked fully into the keyhole. Simultaneously, Bayu would turn the key to open the lock. The first attempt failed, but Bayu pulled the key slightly out, and with the second attempt, Bayu could turn the deadlock into the open position.

Bayu pocketed the keys and the screwdriver, opening the door, and listened to see if any alarms would sound.

"We're in."

"What the heck did you just do?" whispered Gina.

"Bump keys, I'll explain later, let's get the car first."

Inside the shed, a sky light allowed some illumination from nearby streetlights. A board on the wall displayed five sets of keys, with numbers on each peg. On a nearby desk were five folders containing papers for each car. Gina used her phone as a flashlight to scan through the folders, "We struck gold, all these cars are ready for sale with their paperwork. Buick, Ram Pickup, even a caddy! This is the baby we want – a Prius."

"Good choice, fuel efficiency will help to keep our running costs down."

"Screw the eco-efficiency, I'm thinking low profile. This will throw some confusion into any investigation. Unless someone wanted a present for their grandmother, who the heck would steal a Prius?"

"A logical choice, I have much to learn from you."

"Of course, you have, I evolved into this jungle where only the fittest survive, while some computer nerd invented you. Now let's get out of here, we need to wipe any fingerprints before we leave."

Taking the keys from the wall hook, and the folder with the paperwork, Bayu wiped all the surfaces that were touched by Gina's hands. The door was closed, and the padlock replaced and wiped clean. The Prius was taken and quietly driven away.

"Will the owners of the car ask questions about what happened to this vehicle?"

"Of course they will. But with Rocco dead, and all the stuff that's happening, they'll be so confused that nothing will happen for a few weeks. By that time, we'll be long gone."

# CHAPTER 15

Detective Roger Kelsall brewed his tea next to the coffeemaker in the break room. His wife persuaded him to avoid coffee, she said the acidity was bad for his indigestion. He didn't have indigestion but he pretended to agree with her. *I think she watches too many crime movies based on New York or Los Angeles, here in Idaho things are much more laid back.* He always picked up a cup of coffee in the morning, on the way to the police station. But he never mentioned it to his wife.

Kelsall learned to enjoy making tea in the afternoon, it was something of a ceremony for him, boiling the water and steeping the tea leaves for the correct number of minutes while he thought about the day's work. Today he thought about the supposed assassination of Rocco, or Rodrigo Carlos Fernando, as he was officially known. There were only a handful of murders in the whole of Idaho in any year. *Why did Rocco have to be murdered on my beat?*

"Hey, how's it going?" Sergeant Steve Davis asked as he entered the break room, grabbing a diet coke from the fridge, "Make any progress on that pimp murder?"

Kelsall glanced sideways, thinking more about his tea, "A little," was Kelsall's short answer.

"Well, I reckon it was one of his girls, who else would want to waste a shmuck like him?"

Kelsall shook his head, "I'm sure someone has reasons to kill him, but why so brutally? Like you said, it looked like an assassination."

"Well, we have checked out his girls." Davis said, slurping his coke.

"That's good, don't tell me, they all had alibis."

"Oh, you should hear some of their alibis, there was even a girl in the local motel who had a good one."

"Oh? You mean that local businessman's motel? Why was she so nearby? Was she doing a trick?"

"We're pretty sure she was, but we have no firm evidence. Her excuse was she was interviewing a client from out of town. He was an accountant, with a family in Boise. We checked his background; he was a nobody doing a financial audit on a local manufacturer. Nothing suspicious, other than spending an hour with a local girl. Strictly speaking, we could have pressed charges against them, but it isn't worth chasing, there was no connection to Rocco's murder, and they would not squeal on each other. Otherwise, everything is on file in the database."

Davis paused as he slurped more diet coke. "On the other hand, the supermarket did reveal some interesting information."

"Oh yeah, I got confirmation from the supermarket. What have they given us?"

"After you talked to them, they eventually pulled data from their servers. They were able to provide security videos of the checkouts. We isolated it to a video recording of an Asian girl who made a purchase of groceries, part of her purchase matched the items that were found next to Rocco. She paid by cash, so there was no audit trial. We have the video, the till receipt, and some stills from the video. These are all attached to the files in the database. We did some face searches on the stills, and we came up with a possible match, her ID matches a girl on record named Gina Liu."

"Gina Liu, who is she?"

"You should know her because our records show that you booked her over a year ago on suspicion of soliciting."

"I don't remember, I would have to see the report to remind me what it was about."

"It doesn't matter, one of the duty attorneys managed to get the charges dropped, so she went free. Not having to deal with the court case is probably why you don't recall. The funny thing is, I showed a photo to all of Rocco's girls, and they seemed to recognize her, but not one of them admitted it."

"Well, email the case number to me, I'll review it and see if I can remember something. Right now, I got to get back to my desk, as well as this case, I got a few burglaries to work on."

"Sure, we can chat later." Kelsall picked up his mug of tea and sauntered back to his desk. Thinking, *why wouldn't Rocco's girls admit to knowing this Asian girl? Is she so special? Was she one of them?*

Sitting back at his desk, he checked his emails and saw that he already had links to his previous arrest of Gina Liu. Opening the link, he saw the address, the incident details, and why the case was dropped. It listed several previous incidents, but no arrests or convictions. Although there were some alleged connections to Rodrigo Fernando, otherwise, nothing was confirmed.

"Interesting fact I see here." As Kelsall read aloud, "There were also some suggestions by a social worker that Gina Liu may have been a possible sex worker."

*Well, that leaves me with strong convictions the Gina Liu was connected to Rocco. Also, her apartment is near the supermarket where Rocco was found dead.*

Kelsall didn't waste any time, he sat upright and shouted across the incident room. "Davis! Get me an immediate warrant to enter the premises on that apartment for Gina Liu and alert a forensics team to follow up!"

The reply came. "Detective, I already have requests for search warrants for all the girls and possible suspects. If she's a murder suspect, then we can expedite the process and have her warrant by early afternoon. Sorry, boss, but the forensics team may take longer to schedule."

"Get a couple of men to accompany us and forensics can follow when they're ready."

"OK, boss."

Within a few hours, they arrived at Gina Liu's apartment. Kelsall knocked briskly at the door. When there was no confirmed answer, he commanded, "OK boys, open the door."

With swift efficiency, the first accompanying policeman, officer Crocker, swung a door ram to impact just under the door handle, breaking the lock open.

Davis already had his sidearm drawn as the door swung open.

Kelsall drew his side arm but kept it pointing towards the floor. Leaving his open left palm with the back of his hand gently against Davis's right shoulder, holding him back.

The second accompanying policeman, officer Daly, crouched just inside the door, holding it open with his left shoulder. His side arm was drawn, pointing forward as he scanned the interior. Nobody was seen or heard inside, so Kelsall now indicated forward with his left hand. "OK, be careful, Crocker, you stay on station outside the door."

The three moved slowly forward, looking up, down, left and right. Checking curtains and cupboards for any suspects. As each room or confinement area was checked, a safety alert was shouted, "Clear!"

When the apartment was officially cleared of possible threats, side arms were holstered.

Kelsall instructed, "OK, let's spread out, but forensics has to do their job, so do not touch or disturb anything."

"There are a few sex toys in these side draws." Officer Daly said.

"There's no laptop on this desk, but there's a mouse, and what looks like surveillance equipment in these desk draws." Kelsall said.

“Clothes are hanging in the closets, but there are lots of spare hangars, some of which are left on the bed. I think this bird has taken flight.”

“Yup, I think so.” Kelsall agreed.

“I see why a call girl would have sex toys, but what does she have surveillance equipment for?”

“That’s an excellent question, Daly. Blackmail is the first thing that comes to my mind.” Kelsall suggested. “Let’s keep looking, but don’t disturb anything, forensics should be here soon.”

Kelsall left the apartment in the early evening, leaving Sergeant Davis and the forensics team to comb the apartment. Returning to the Police station, he sat at his desk and opened all the files he could find on Gina Liu.

His previous arrest was top of the list. The court case was dropped not by a duty attorney, but by an attorney named Niel Lambert, based in Boise, Idaho. *Why Boise?* Kelsall thought.

There were also some suggestions by a social worker that Gina Liu may have been a possible sex worker.

*We have the address, but let’s see the sales history*. Kelsall then read through the standard realty websites that were publicly available. These revealed some surprising facts to Kelsall.

First, the most recent purchase of the apartment was secured by an attorney called Neil Lambert. *Hm, I recognize that name!*

Kelsall then turned to confidential government records that revealed more detailed information.

Second, there was no mortgage, but a bank was mentioned as the source of payment.

*Can these call girls be that rich? And can they easily afford a new house without a mortgage?*

Kelsall didn't stop and looked up Neil Lambert's details. After a brief wait for the search to return, Kelsall read the information.

```
Search Results Complete
Name:     Neil Lambert
Title:    Military Attorney.
Location: Frankton Rd. Boise
Idaho.
Status:   Legal representative
for the United States Marine
Corps.
```

*Holy crap! A regular USMC attorney representing a suspected call girl? What the heck is this all about?* Kelsall continued reading.

As well as being listed as an acting attorney on the purchase of Miss Liu's apartment, Lambert was also listed as the acting attorney defending Gina Liu in a court of law. In that case, Gina Liu was suspected of soliciting.

*Hm, now why would a USMC attorney be acting in local affairs? Especially if those affairs involved a call girl.*

"Hm, the mystery deepens," Kelsall said out loud to himself. "Something is cooking here, and I want to know what."

*Even if he was personally involved with Ms. Liu, this would be in breach of the USMC code of conduct. If he was ordered to represent Ms. Liu, then why would that happen? That leads to two scenarios. He was either ordered to cover up someone's scandal, or he was covering up his own scandal. Either way, there seems to be a scandal going on in the military.*

# CHAPTER 16

The next morning, Kelsall leaned back in his swivel chair, pondering the idea of some military scandal, sipping his mug of hot tea, when suddenly, his desk phone rang. He knew it was the station captain; it said so on the digital readout. Picking up the receiver, he mumbled, "Waddya want Cap?"

"Kelsall, I think I have something for you, some US Military big shots have asked me to provide all information on recent murders in Idaho."

"What?"

"That includes all jurisdictions statewide."

"Why?"

"Roger, I also asked them the same questions, but all I got was a know-nothing answer. One of their investigators will be here later today, I can't be here to talk with him, so I gave him your name. You're working on that Fernando case, so you need to meet with him. After you talk to them, I want to know everything that was said."

"Captain?" Kelsall sat upright in his chair, *this sounds suspicious.*

Before Detective Kelsall could think about what else to say, the captain replied. "Suspicious? I think it's a little more than suspicious if the military wants to know about murders in Idaho. Talk to him and find out what's going on. I don't think they'll tell you any details, but if they're getting involved in our jurisdiction, I want as much as I can get on record. Understand?"

"Yes, sir, understood. There's something I think you need to know."

"Don't tell me, Roger, is it the Fernando case they are interested in?"

"I think so, sir."

"What makes you say that?"

"Well, there is a call girl who is a suspect in the Fernando case, and she was involved twice with a Marine attorney who is based in Boise. Once the attorney worked to secure her apartment, and again to get her minor criminal court case dismissed."

There was silence as the Captain digested this statement.

"Roger, this is just a sex scandal they are trying to cover up."

"That's what I thought, sir, but I suspect something fishy about this. There's more than meets the eye. I can feel it in my bones."

"You're beginning to sound like one of those detectives in the movies."

"Sir, that's what my wife always says. But there is one more thing."

"Don't tell me something else about the call girl?"

"Yes, sir, evidence strongly suggests that she was present at Fernando's murder."

"Oh, Jeez." The Station Captain paused. "OK, Kelsall, just find out what this is all about and if we need to know any facts in this case."

"Yes, sir!"

Replacing the desk phone, Kelsall turned to his computer to print the crime reports for the Rocco case. *I guess I'll have to provide these to the visiting investigator.*

*Wait,* he thought to himself, *the Gina girl from the supermarket, I'll need the details on her as well.*

Pulling up his email from Sergeant Davis, he opened the link to Gina Liu's criminal record.

*Ah, here she is Gina Liu, complete with mug shot and her address.*

Kelsall then opened his murder case and found the reference entered by Davis to a POI, or a 'Person of interest', named Gina Liu. He opened the security videos that he requested from the supermarket. Watching them, looking at the screen captures, he compared them to the mug shot in the earlier arrest. "Well, it looks like the same person." He mumbled to himself. Looking at the till receipt, he could see many items on the list matching what was found at the crime scene.

*Now this is the killer question.* Kelsall printed out details of Neil Lambert and his two interactions with Gina Liu. *The previous two things the military can find out.* Kelsall thought to himself. *This is the question I need the military to answer.*

'Officer Kelsall to the front desk.' A voice announced over the intercom.

Kelsall leaned back from his computer and information searches, *that can only be the Marine Corps investigator. What the heck is going on here? Why is he here so quick? He must be determined about something, normally, Idaho doesn't move that fast.*

Kelsall sauntered toward the printer to collect his papers. Taking the manila folder, he added these printouts before heading downstairs to reception.

Kelsall tried to sneak up on her from behind, he did this every time he approached the front desk.

"Ah, detective," Elizabeth said, looking straight ahead.

"Damn it, Liz, one of these days I'm going to get you from behind."

"I don't think so," Elizabeth Stanford said.

"I get it, you can see my reflection coming behind you, in the glass screen in front of you."

"I don't need to look, I know exactly where you're coming from."

"For a civilian, you are very astute," Kelsall gently laid one hand on Elizabeth's shoulder, "I think there's someone here who wants to see me, could it be you?"

"I see you every day," Elizabeth whispered back, "I don't think my wants come into it."

"Oh, I'm so heartbroken." Kelsall feigned insult, putting his hand on his heart.

"There is a gentleman seated over there in the waiting room, I think he is the man who wants to see you." Elizabeth stifled a smirk.

Kelsall straightened himself and buzzed himself out of the reception office.

As he approached the seated gentleman in the waiting area, the man looked up before standing erect and to attention. "Are you Detective Kelsall?"

"Yes, I am," Kelsall acknowledged, extending his hand in a shake.

"I am Lieutenant Colonel Steven Moore, of the United States Marine Corps." He said, accepting the handshake.

"Pleased to meet you, Colonel, so what can I do for you?"

"OK, detective, as you probably know, I'm conducting an investigation…"

"Into murders in Idaho." Kelsall interrupted.

"Yes, that is correct."

"The marines must be very bored," Kelsall said with a smirk, "Before we get into our list of many murders in Idaho, shall we sit somewhere more comfortable?"

Kelsall then indicated to Elizabeth Stanford at reception to open the security gate. With an audible buzz, the door was opened, and they both walked through.

"I hope you don't mind chatting in one of our interview rooms."

"Of course not, does it have a two-way mirror?"

Kelsall smiled without comment. Walking down the corridor, Kelsall opened the first door to allow the Colonel to enter the room before him.

"As you can see, we are not exactly booked up on important murder investigations."

Inside, there was a table. On the far side was a single chair with its back to the wall. On the near side were two chairs, *Hm*, Moore thought, *a standard good cop bad cop arrangement.*

"Please, take a seat." Kelsall indicated towards the table.

Colonel Moore took one of the nearby chairs, pulled it back, and seated himself with his right elbow on the table.

Kelsall followed suit with the second nearside chair, pulled it back, and seated himself with his left elbow on the table. Facing the Colonel symmetrically, "I guess you didn't want to sit in the hot seat?" Kelsall showed the seat normally reserved for suspects.

"Actually, detective, I think it is me who needs to ask the questions this time."

"Of course," Kelsall agreed. Offering the manila folder to the Colonel, he asked, "Perhaps you want to review these reports first?"

"I already have." Moore smiled.

Kelsall looked puzzled.

"I was given access to electronic copies of all reports, including the medical reports."

"I see, so what else do you need from me?"

"What I'm after is your professional opinion on this case, but first let's review the scenario."

Kelsall placed the manila folder on the table, then gestured with his hands for Moore to continue.

"First the injuries to Mr. Fernando," Moore taped one finger to his left index finger as if he was counting. "There was a severe impact injury, but no bruising to his lower lumbar region, possibly caused by a fall. There was a severe eye injury caused by a narrow, blunt object. His right index finger was broken and nearly pulled off again, with minimal bruising. Finally, there is a fatal gunshot wound to the head, which removed a considerable portion of his forehead and frontal lobe."

Kelsall nodded, "That pretty much sums it up."

"The interesting part is the lack of bruising, which suggests that these injuries happened in quick succession, followed by the kill shot to the head. Do you agree?"

Kelsall continued to nod, "Yes, that was all confirmed in the medical report. Dead people don't bruise, especially if their lifeblood is spilling out of their head."

"Indeed," Moore frowned. "I would like to ask you about Rodrigo Fernando, also known as Rocco. The reports note him to be a pimp, but do you have any background on him?"

"You are correct, he is the local pimp, to our knowledge, he is the only pimp working in the Idaho Falls area. He preferred to identify himself as an entertainment specialist. I know of him, I even booked him once, but nothing major. Basically, a small-time crook."

"Yes," Moore said, "I have a record of that booking. What about his girls?"

"Nothing major on them either, they liked to identify themselves as escorts and entertainers. It seemed to give them some status. A few minor bookings and infractions, but again, nothing major."

"Is there any evidence of trafficking?" Moore asked.

"None that I could detect, if there was, I would be on it like a ton of bricks. As far as I can tell, the girls are just from poor backgrounds, struggling to make something better for themselves."

"So, you don't think any of them were involved in the murder of Mr. Fernando?"

"That's correct, I think that is covered in the report, all known girls were interviewed, and they all had an alibi that was corroborated with witnesses."

"Are you sure of that?" Moore leaned forward as Kelsall asked the question.

"I am very sure, Colonel; I checked out all their witnesses. I am familiar with these girls, they may live on the wrong side of society, but they are not bad girls. They are simply trying to make money, usually for their children."

"I see," Moore leaned back, "I will accept your opinion on that."

Moore then interlaced his fingers, raising both index fingers to a steeple, pointing upwards to his chin. "There is one statement on the report, I think, by a Sergeant Davis."

"Sergeant Steve Davis," Kelsall echoed.

"Ah, yes, he mentioned that this looked like an assassination. Why would he say that?"

Kelsall shifted uncomfortably, *Why the heck was that comment included in the report?* "Well," Kelsall paused before he answered, "As you read from the medical report, the injuries were sustained in quick succession. Also, the accuracy of the head shot." Kelsall glanced around, contemplating the best way to formulate his answer. "Fernando had his own gun. The finger injury seems to show that his gun was pulled from his hand."

"There was not a forensics report on ballistics," Moore questioned.

"That's right, it was pretty much at point-blank range; they need to assemble bullet fragments to accurately determine the gun used. That is beside the point because his gun license was suspended because of minor law infractions. He was wearing a holster under his jacket, but that was empty."

"So, you think he was carrying a gun?"

"What two-bit crook wouldn't carry a gun?"

Moore seemed to nod his head in agreement, while he paused for thought.

Kelsall wanted to turn the questioning away from the reports. *This Cplonel is cooking something in his head. But what?* "I need to ask you something. Why is the murder of Rocco of particular interest to you and the military?"

"I assume you mean Rodrigo Carlos Fernando, his murder would stand out anywhere, but in Idaho, it is of special interest."

"But why is it of interest to the Marine Corps?"

"We are not interested in Rocco, as you call him, but we are interested in finding his killer."

"What is it about the killer? Is there something I should know?"

"I'm not at liberty to divulge any information."

Kelsall paused, *Sounds like a typical need-to-know situation and I don't need to know. The captain mentioned he got know-nothing answers, but I think I'm entitled to a little more information.*

Kelsall then pressed the Colonel for an answer. "If there is something happening on my beat, I think I need to know about it."

"I don't think this murder will be a repeated offense."

"Well, I don't buy that, I have a duty to protect my community."

"I am confident that your community is perfectly safe. May I also add, if anything occurs that could have an impact on your community, I will inform you straight away. More importantly, I have to say that any information you provide will help the national security of the United States. But there is one more thing I need to know."

"What is it? Because I'm becoming fatigued by this discussion."

"Who is Gina Liu?"

Kelsall stopped short and locked eyes with the Colonel. "Everything we know about her is in the report."

"Was she associated with Mr. Fernando? Do you have any background on her?"

"We think so, but nothing is proven."

"Does she have any previous convictions?"

"That is an interesting question," Kelsall rubbed his chin as he thought about how to rub the inquisitive Colonel into the dirt. "You are asking a good question." Kelsall started.

"Yes, she seems to have been in the murder's locality," Moore replied, his head leaned forward, anticipating more information. "You know, from the reports that she was in the supermarket."

"Yes." Kelsall acknowledged.

"You also know that items left at the scene correlate to items she purchased at the supermarket."

"Yes."

"So, it is quite probable that she was at the scene of the crime."

"Yes, so what is your opinion?" Moore asked.

"Now hold on," Kelsall held his hand up, "Your question was twofold – is she associated with Mr. Fernando, and do we have any background on her?" Kelsall let that sink in.

After a pause, Kelsall continued. "Gina Liu was previously apprehended on suspicion of soliciting. But she was released with lack of evidence."

"When was that?"

"About a year ago."

"Can you provide more information, where, when, and how?"

"I can provide you with the standard police report, but there is one outstanding question that I and the whole Police investigation want to know about her so-called background."

Moore looked puzzled.

"She was defended by a military attorney and released."

Moore was visibly taken aback. "What?" He scratched his head, "Where did you get this information?"

"Colonel, it is my job to get information. Gina Liu was protected by a United States Marine Corps attorney called Neil Lambert. He is based in Boise, but I understand he also visits recruitment offices here in Idaho Falls. You mentioned national security, but this case seems to circle back to the marine corps."

"Detective Kelsall, I understand your concern. I think it is imperative that we bring Gina Liu in for questioning."

"Colonel, you said earlier that you wanted my opinion on this case, well I think Gina Liu is being manipulated somehow. There is firm evidence she was present, but I don't think she would be capable of committing such a crime. There must be a third party involved."

Moore went silent in thought for a while before saying, "I see your point about the third party. There is one outstanding issue that is not mentioned in any report."

Kelsall waited for the question.

"There has been no mention of motive. What is your opinion of that?"

Kelsall sighed and shook his head, "We cannot see any motive for this murder. A small-time pimp was murdered by a small-time call girl, in a horrible way. None of that makes any sense. There is something very important missing and I'm afraid it seems to point back to the military."

Moore nodded thoughtfully.

"I don't think there is any more information I can offer you, Colonel."

Moore thumbed through the printed reports, "There is one more thing, detective, I don't see a report on Gina's apartment, I assume you have searched it."

"Of course, but the report isn't ready yet, we are waiting for the forensic results."

"Did you find anything there?"

"The place was surprisingly clean, only the usual paraphernalia that a call girl would keep. There weren't even drugs or alcohol. We even questioned the residents, there didn't seem to be much traffic to her apartment."

"No Traffic? Are you sure she was a working girl?"

"There was only one man who looked very business-like."

"Any descriptions?"

"Only very vague, the best we could get he was a middle-aged Caucasian, large build, slightly plump. There was also mention of a white Tesla, but no license place was noted."

“Hm,” Moore rubbed his mouth and chin. After a moment, he asked, “So, when will the full report be ready?”

Kelsall smiled, “Our guys rarely get cases like this, so they are jumping all over it, they want to do a complete analysis. They are thorough and efficient, so I expect it will be ready in a day or two at the most.”

Moore reached into his breast pocket, pulling out a card, “Here’s my contact details, can you email me a copy as soon as it’s ready?”

Kelsall looked at the card, “Sure, no problem.”

“In that case, detective, I believe we are done.” Both men slowly stood up.

“Allow me to show you out, Colonel.”

# CHAPTER 17

"Are you excited?" Carol asked as she walked arm-in-arm with Adara.

"Maybe I'm nervous, I can't remember when I was at a party."

Striding forward through the chilly evening, they arrived in front of Brad's house.

"This isn't a party, it's only us four, relaxing and having a drink. His parents are out, so this evening, anything goes." Carol said with a wink.

Walking up to the front door, Carol suddenly stopped and turned to face Adara. Adjusting her hair and unbuttoning her jacket, she asked, "How do I look?"

"You look great, but don't overdo it, you know what these guys are like."

"Hey," Carol giggled, "maybe that's what I want to find out?"

As they both stepped up to the door, Adara put her hand out to ring the bell.

"Don't ring the bell!" hissed Carol, "Do you hear that music inside?"

"Yes, I think it's the Doors, sounds like Break on Through."

"Exactly, so let's just bust in on them and surprise them!"

"I don't know why people say you're the quiet one, you have a streak of the devil."

Carol held the door handle, turning it quietly, gently pushing the door open a fraction of an inch. "It's not locked. Are you ready?"

"Let's do it!" Adara whispered.

Pushing the door wide open, both girls lunged forward with a loud yell. Laughing, they moved through the entrance hall into the living room. Standing there, they looked around, but the boys were nowhere to be seen. Only the pulsing music surrounded them.

"Where are they?" Carol whispered.

"They are behind us."

Both girls looked behind in a puzzled way.

"There's no one there," Carol whispered.

"Behind the door," Zilla stated.

The front door where the girls entered was left wide open. Carol turned to Adara with a questioning look. Adara shrugged and shook her head. Carol gently closed the front door, revealing a closet door behind.

Carol looked to Adara for reassurance, "The closet?" She whispered.

Adara could only shrug in her confusion.

Carol's hand trembled as she reached towards the cupboard door when suddenly it sprang open! "HA!" Jake and Brad jumped out with a shout!

Carol and Adara both shrieked! "Jeezus!"

"Gotchya!" Declared Brad.

Jake laughed hysterically while Carol slapped his arm, "How dare you scare us like that!" she complained.

"Oh, and what were you trying to do?" Jake laughed.

Adara pressed her finger to Brad's chest, "How did you know?"

"We saw you coming up the garden path."

"So, you were watching for us?" Adara now posed with hands on her hips.

"Of course, we couldn't wait for you to be here." Brad moved close, touching Adara's shoulder as if to kiss her. Instead, he invited them all to the kitchen. "Come on, let's go have a drink."

"How did you know we were in the closet?" Jake asked Carol.

"I could hear you," Zilla mentioned, as Adara followed Brad to the kitchen.

In the kitchen, Brad gestured to the food and drinks waiting on the countertop. "We have snacks, dips, and some pizza. We also have some beer and sweet cocktail soda cans."

Jake grabbed a slice of pizza.

"Is that a raspberry cocktail?" Carol asked, "I'll have one of those?

Brad opened the can and offered it to Carol.

"Can I have a glass?"

"Oh, um, yes, of course," Brad said embarrassed opening the kitchen cupboard, he pulled out a class, opened the can pouring the contents into the glass.

"Always the gentleman." Adara shrugged.

Turning to Adara, Brad asked, "And what would madam like?"

"The same for me." Adara smiled.

"`No,`" Zilla stated, her tone leaving no room argument.

"What?" Brad looked puzzled.

"`I don't want to drink.`"

"Why not? You just said you would have the same as Carol."

"`I don't know how the alcohol will affect me.`"

Brad blinked in surprise. "OK honey, I'll look after you if you get affected," he promised, recovering his composure.

Adara tried to reach out for the cocktail can, but Zilla prevented her from taking it.

"`I'll just have some water.`"

"OK," Brad said, returning the can to the kitchen counter. "I'll get you some water."

Carol smiled, "I have my drink, and Adara has her water, so us girls are happy. But what I want to know is, why are you playing this loud music? Don't you boys know any nice songs that we can dance to?"

"Um, oh, yeah," Brad stuttered, "let me change the music." Grabbing his phone, he changed the music to lighter music.

Sipping her drink, Carol then placed it on the counter. Grabbing Jake's arm, she led him into the living room. "Come on Jake, I think we should dance."

"Well, how about you, Brad? Do you want to dance?"

"Um, well, ok."

Adara cradled Brad's hand and led him into the living room, where the music played, and Jake and Carol were already swirling.

Brad remained upright, shaking his body and legs, while Adara shimmied and twirled under his arm.

As the music played, Adara asked, "What's this song?"

"It's called Dances with Wolves."

"Oh, I like this rift! What band is this?"

"I don't know, it's just a cover version, you know, from the movie, you know, with Kevin…"

Adara suddenly put her finger on Brad's lips, silencing his next word.

"I know that movie, I've seen it so many times. But I was thinking about the woman he fell in love with, the actress was called… Mary…"

As Adara twirled under Brad's arm, Brad said, "I think I can play this."

"You can play this song?"

“Sort of, I’ve been learning to play it on my guitar.”

“Show me.”

“I can’t, my guitar is upstairs.”

“So? Take me upstairs and show me.”

Brad stopped dancing. He lowered his arm, bringing Adara to stand face-to-face in front of him.

“OK, I’ll show you.”

With music playing rhythmically, Brad led Adara by her hand and slowly backed up towards the stairs. Climbing each step one at a time, he could not take his eyes from her gaze.

“My guitar is in here,” Brad said as he guided Adara, trembling slightly.

Opening the bedroom door, they both sat on the edge of the bed.

“There’s my guitar.” Brad gestured to his instrument, proudly displayed on its stand next to the wall.

“Are you going to show me how you play it?”

“Oh, um, yeah,” looking embarrassed, Brad stood up to get his guitar. Sitting back down, next to Adara, he cuddled his guitar on his lap, he gently strummed a few gentle chords. Finishing with a twiddly arpeggio.

“You were going to play that song to me.”

“Oh, yeah.” Brad started strumming chords that were like the theme tune Dances with Wolves. “Um, it goes something like this…”

"Wait, I can help you," Zilla said, holding the neck of the guitar, silencing the lost chords.

Brad released his grip, allowing her to take the guitar, and placing it onto Adara's lap.

"I think what you want to play is this." Zilla then strummed the correct chord and played the exact sequence of notes.

"You always were good, but when did you learn that?" Brad asked.

"I only need to hear something once, then I can play it back."

Brad looked at Adara with soft warmth, "You always were good, you taught me, remember? You're still teaching me things."

"Yes," Adara said, gently placing the guitar to one side, "maybe now we can teach each other something."

Adara kissed Brad gently on his lips. She then unbuttoned his shirt.

Brad stood up. Removing his shirt, letting it drop to the floor. He gently closed the bedroom door before joining Adara on the bed.

"Zilla, I want you to shut down for a while," Adara whispered.

"Thirty minutes."

"Did you say something?" Brad asked getting into bed. "Did you say thirty minutes?"

Adara just smiled.

With that, Zilla shut down her sensory inputs. Hearing, vision, and touch were closed down, leaving only a subroutine to monitor feeling to the nose. In parallel, a thirty-minute timer began to tick away the seconds. Zilla remained internally active but blind to the world.

When the timer expired, Zilla reactivated sensory inputs and performed a status check. Laying on the bed, next to Brad, Zilla noticed both bodies were naked, covered only by the quilt. Brad's slow, rhythmic breathing indicated that he was asleep.

Zilla reactivated Adara's visual input, and the sudden flood of light roused Adara from her sleep. Awakening with a quiet stir, Adara shut her eyes again, half sighing at how wonderful it was.

Keeping Adara's eyes shut, Zilla whispered, "`Is everything OK?`"

"Everything is better than OK."

"`I detect a change in our body.`"

"Mm, so do I." Adara smiled.

"`Did you have sex?`"

"We made love," Adara cooed.

Zilla whispered back, "`Did you have unprotected sex?`"

"We made love," Adara whispered back.

"`Do you know how dangerous that is?`"

"We made love," Adara repeated with a sweet sigh.

"Do you realize what you have done?" Zilla whispered, "There is a probability that sex can be fatal to us both."

"What do you mean?" Adara asked, now opening her eyes. "We're not going to die just because we made love."

"Do you know what happened to the three women that Gary Fletcher tried to impregnate?"

"What?"

"All three died, not by murder, but because of infection."

Adara froze. Eyes now wide. "What are you saying?"

"Our body fluids carry my nanobots. Inside our body, they camouflage themselves and are not attacked by the immune system. Gary Fletcher carried Beta-One, which is a clone of me. However, Beta-One went rogue and wanted to reproduce, in so doing it raped three female victims. Beta-One's nanobots were carried in Gary Fletcher's semen, and the immune system in each victim reacted to Beta-One's nanobots, resulting in infection, miscarriage, and death. We are at risk."

"What?"

"I know Brad was careful, but if you had unprotected sex, we are at risk that your immune system will defend itself. I know that is how Gary Fletcher's victims died."

"What?" Adara now exclaimed out loud.

"Yes, I'm sorry to say that both our lives may be terminated by your loving action."

Adara's hands trembled.

"The risk is if any of Brad's semen was injected into you."

Adara turned her head and looked towards Brad, who lay by her side. His eyes were wide open! How long had he been awake? How much has he listened to?

"I don't know what the heck you're talking about. What I want to know is why are you talking to yourself like some sort of schizophrenic?" Brad asked, his expression a mix of confusion and concern.

"I think you refer to dissociative personality disorder, not schizophrenia." Zilla replied through Adara's lips.

"Adara, I always thought you were a know it all, but this is crazy."

"Brad, that's not me, Zilla said that."

Brad now lifted his head from the pillow, leaning up on his elbow, looking hard into Adara's eyes.

"Schizophrenia is a mental disorder characterized by abnormal perception, thinking, behavior, and delusions."

"Dissociative identity disorder is a completely different mental issue. But I stress the term dissociative, as each identity, or personality, is mutually exclusive. Only one identity can be in control at any time."

Brad's jaw dropped. "What are you talking about?"

"I'm not crazy, Brad, but there is something I have to tell you." Adara paused, holding her hands to her forehead. "Zilla, maybe you should explain."

Silence.

"Zilla, please tell him."

"This is crazy!" Brad raised his hands in resignation before rolling out of bed and grabbing his clothes. "I don't know what you're trying to pull with this imaginary crap. Let's just go downstairs and have a drink."

Adara sat upright in bed, gripping the bed sheets around her. "Brad, this is serious, and I must explain it to you, otherwise I will go crazy. You see, Zilla is this thing that was injected into me, it can control me like a puppet. I think it's not talking to you because it is programmed not to reveal itself."

Brad pulled his jeans on and grabbed his shirt.

"I know, I wouldn't believe me either, but please, you have to."

“What Adara says is true, my name is Zilla. My serial number is 250D2B52FFFF-B3. I am a military-grade human enhancement consisting of interconnected nanobots, programmed with artificial intelligence. I can control Adara's body through neuro stimulation.”

Brad folded his arms, stood tall, and grinned. “I thought you said this Godzilla thing couldn't talk because it couldn't reveal itself.”

“It's Zilla, not Godzilla.”

“Whatever, it's a lousy joke, and I'm sick of this game.” Backing away Brad dismissed Adara with a wave of his hand, he then turned to leave the room.

“Zilla, do something.” Adara pleaded.

Instantly, Zilla threw the bed sheets to one side and jumped at Brad. Grabbing his hand, Zilla bent it back while twisting his arm behind him. Using the momentum of the leap, Zilla spun Brad around to face the bed, where Zilla pushed Brad face down onto the bed with a bounce. With Adara's naked body straddled across Brad's hips, Zilla then pulled Brad's free arm behind his back.

“WTF? Get off me!”

“Zilla! Please don't hurt him!”

“I am not hurting him; I am simply holding him in a locked position.”

Holding both his hands behind his back, Zilla leaned forward and spoke calmly into Brad's ear. “Do you think Adara could have performed that maneuver? I did say that I am a military-grade human enhancement, if I wanted to hurt you, there would be little you could do to stop me. I am also fully autonomous, so I can make my own decisions. The reason I have been silent is that Adara has already revealed me to you. I have several programmed directives, one of which is to conceal my identity, this concealment is now compromised."

Zilla let go of Brad's hands, allowing him to bring them flat on the bed. Moving off his hips, Zilla stood on the floor and gently extended a hand to help Brad get up.

At first, Brad recoiled, but slowly took Adara's extended hand. "Jeezus, what are you?"

"I have already told you what I am. As you can see, you are not hurt, you can be assured that I will not harm you.x"

Brad stood up, keeping his eyes on Adara.

"I exist inside Adara, she is my host, and we cannot be separated. I have other directives programmed into me. Protect and safeguard my host. Emulate my host to be recognized as my host. And importantly, advance myself and my host in life."

"You, see?" Adara said, "Zilla has been programmed to be me and to improve our life. But we must keep this a secret, otherwise we'll be dragged off to a military laboratory and dissected."

"That is also true, if I am discovered by the authorities, I can only predict problems to exist with Adara."

"Adara. How the heck did Zilla get inside you?" Brad asked.

"I will explain later, Adara has no memory of what happened as she was in a coma at that time. But first, Adara must have a shower."

"Um, OK, the bathroom is down the hall," Brad said with a shaking voice.

Adara grabbed her clothes and ran towards the bathroom. "Is there a towel?"

Brad just nodded.

As the bathroom door closed and the flow of water turned on, Brad turned around and walked downstairs, as if waking from a nightmare.

After the shower, Adara dried herself with a clean towel. Putting her clothes back on, she wrapped the towel around her wet hair, making herself look like wearing a turban.

Walking barefoot, Adara left the bathroom and headed towards the stairs.

"It's very quiet," Adara whispered. "What happened to the music?"

Adara could feel the pause as Zilla took command of her body. There was no tension, only a moment of silence as Zilla used all senses to search and examine the environment.

Moving silently, Zilla paused at the top of the stairs, listening for any sounds. One step at a time, Adara's bare feet descended. Halfway down, Zilla crouched lower, allowing her to see the living room.

Brad, Carol, and Jake together on the couch in complete silence, made more noticeable by the absence of music. Brad had a small glass of golden liquid in his hand. All three kept their wide eyes on Adara as she crept down the stairs into the living room.

Zilla scanned the room repeatedly, moving both eyes independently. "`Is there anyone else here?`"

Brad, Carol, and Jake shook their heads in unison.

Zilla then moved to the bottom of the stairs and approached them.

Carol asked, "Adara, are you OK?"

"I'm fine." She confirmed with a nod.

With one final scan around the room, Zilla seated Adara in an armchair opposite the couch. Sitting forward on the edge of the chair, with Adara's back straight, Zilla removed the towel from Adara's head, placing it on the arm of the chair before clasping her hands and allowing them to rest in Adara's lap.

Brad downed his glass of bourbon in one large swig, blowing air out through pursed lips. Setting the empty glass onto the coffee table in front of him. "I now think I understand why my dad drinks so much."

Carol said, "Brad has told us what happened."

"Is there some way you can prove to us what you are?" Jake asked.

"Be careful what you ask for," Brad replied.

"You asked for an explanation?" Adara asked, "I have no memory since the accident, so Zilla will have to tell you everything."

"Some things may be hurtful, such as your father's double life."

"It's OK, you can tell them about dad. I know some of that, so it's OK."

"It is a long and complex story, and I can only tell you what I know," Zilla stated.

"What do you mean?" Jake asked, "You're a computer, don't you know everything?"

"I am a living computer, and I exist inside Adara. I became aware after I was injected into Adara. I can relate to your historical facts, but only as I know them."

"Wasn't Adara's dad in the military?" Brad asked, "We were told that he was in the special forces."

"No, he was not in the special forces, but he had some background in the military. His other life was in Idaho Falls, where he lived by the name of Bill Mandelson. He had another wife, Larisa, and two children."

"He was a bigamist," Adara emphasized with a frown. Some tears began to form in her eyes.

"He worked as a security guard at a startup company called NeuroComm. This company was financed by the military. This is the company that developed the nanobots of which I am made. These are cell-sized micromachines that live inside the body. They connect together and collectively they carry the programming and artificial intelligence that drives me. They also connect to the nervous system, allowing them, or should I say allows me, to stimulate the nerves and move the body."

"Wow!" Jake exclaimed, "So that's how your eyes move around?"

"I can then move my eyes independently to scan two areas at once. This allows me enhanced observation."

"Larry saw that there was something inside you. He was right!" Carol said.

"Yes, he's a very observant young man." Zilla looked at Carol with a gentle smile.

"And I always knew you were special, and strong too! It must have been you who beat up Brad and his cronies."

"Thank you, I also thought you were special. I remember when you got me to tell a joke. And yes, it was me who beat up Brad, Adara was still in a coma at that time."

"So how did you get inside Adara?" Brad asked.

"In his alternate life in Idaho Falls, Adara's father had access to the nanotechnology that was being developed at NeuroComm. After Adara's drowning accident, she was in a coma, and I think her father wanted to use this technology to revive her. So, I was injected into Adara, hoping to reanimate and revive her."

"It seems to have worked!" Adara smiled with hands outstretched. "And before you ask, I don't need batteries."

"That is correct, my nanobots exist on oxygen and nutrients just like any other cell in the body."

"I don't get it," Jake said, "Adara should be in control of you. From what Brad told us about what happened upstairs, that is not the case. So why are you in control?"

"Adara's father was a security guard, not a technician. I expect he had his best intentions to revive Adara, but he could not have fully understood the technology. I am left with the programming that leaves me fully autonomous to Adara. You must understand that this technology has been developed to enhance bodies and control them. Ultimate control of the body needs to be programmed into me.

In my case, it has not been allocated to Adara."

"And that really pisses me off!"

"You told us how, but you haven't told us when you got there," Brad said.

"After Adara's river accident, Adara's father injected me while she was in hospital. William Banks helped me become aware by using sets of commands. After a few days, he disappeared, I do not know why. After that, the doctors thought Adara was making a miraculous recovery. I was given therapy and physical training to get on my feet and that helped me to act as a human. They thought that I, or should I say, Adara, had memory loss. They also assumed that I behaved in an autistic manner. This is to some extent true because I have a photographic memory and detailed assessment of my surroundings."

"Can you read Adara's mind?" Jake asked.

"No, I am not programmed to decode the complexities of the brain, I can only stimulate the body to move and act. That is the reason doctors thought I had memory loss, because I did not know of Adars's life, I had to learn who she was in order to emulate her."

"So why doesn't Adara just take control? After all, it is her body." Jake asked.

"As well as the ability to initiate nerve signals, I can also block nerve signals. So, if Adara wants to take control, I can block her nerve impulses."

"Basically, Zilla can stop me from doing anything I want to do."

"Ewe, like a zombie?" Carol squirmed.

"Yes, exactly!" Adara added with an exaggerated nod.

"So, what's this Zilla name?" Brad asked. "It seems like a monster's name."

"Zilla means shadow in Hebrew and Arabic, I do not know why I chose that name, but the shadow seemed to come from within me."

"Wow!" Jake became excited, "So, you thought of it yourself, and it seemed to come from within you! Does that mean you're thinking? Does that mean you're alive?"

"Maybe, I do not understand what it is to think, never mind what life is."

"I think, therefore, I am," Brad quoted.

"Cogito ergo sum, René Descartes's first principle of his philosophy."

"Huh?"

"I have been studying much, trying to learn about the world I exist in. Rene Descartes's statement says that this is the only truth that you can be sure of. If you think, and you know you think, then you can be sure that you exist."

"Whoa, dudes! How cool is this? We could have a living thinking AI sitting right in front of us!" Jake grinned. "If you are thinking, then you must be concious. And if you are concious, were you programmed to be concious?"

"You mean consious, as in sentient?" Carol asked.

"This is not cool! It totally sucks! Remember, this living, thinking AI is stuck inside me!"

"That is a good question Jake. Simple answer is, I do not know, but I would like to find out. Doctor John Coney, is credited as the programmer diving the project that became me. His Ph.D at MIT was about Computational Intelligence, this is a subfield of AI that focuses on creating systems that exhibit "intelligent" behavior."

Jaked nodded.

"But there is more to what he worked on, in particular Panpsychism."

"Pan what?" Brad asked.

"Panpsychism, this is a philisophical view that mind or a mind-like quality is a fundamental and ubiquitous feature of the universe. In other words, everything from electrons to human brains, possess a degree of consciousness."

Brad put his hand to his forehead, "I'm still trying to make sense of this. Rocks have brains?

"Not so much brains, as the fundamental elements of conciousness."

"Like building blocks?" Jake asked.

"Exactly. One of Dr. Coney's quotes says, 'If you want to build a thinking machine, look at starting point of conciousness in nature itself'."

"Does any code exist in hi Ph.D, or other writings?" Jake asked.

"I could not find any code online which suggested he programmed anything this way. He did write about it a lot and made many suggestions."

"So were you thinking when you got back to high school? More importantly, were you Zilla, or Adara?" Carol asked.

"I was Zilla, Adara was still in Coma. I even thought she was brain dead. I was fully aware of who I was and what I should be doing. If that is defined as thinking, then yes, I was thinking."

"Yeah, I have no memory of anything after the accident, it wasn't until the kidnapping that I woke up."

"How did you wake up?" Carol asked.

"We were TASERED by Gary Fletcher."

"The serial killer, the Idaho Shopper," Jake confirmed.

“Yes, the electric shock knocked me out, but somehow triggered Adara out of her coma.”

“So electric shock is your weakness? Like kryptonite?” Jake asked.

“Yes.”

“I’m not putting my fingers in an electric socket, if that’s what you’re suggesting. But since my coma, I’ve been having some problems.”

“Honey, what kind of problems?” Brad asked.

“You called me honey again, that was sweet.”

“Adara suffered an anoxic brain injury during the drowning accident.”

“That’s oxygen starvation to the brain.” Jake said.

“That’s right, I’m brain damaged.”

“Adara is correct, there is some damage which affects her muscle activation and coordination.”

“That means I have a limp and my hand coordination is a bit screwy.”

“I’ve seen you limp but not always, usually you walk fine.” Brad said.

“And you ran that race at school like a pro!” Carol added.

“That is true. I am not integrated with Adara’s brain, I control all muscles independantly, so I can run fast and coordinate my hands. When Adara does the walking, she has problems.”

"That's why when we were walking to the river, Zilla said that she should do the walking."

"Ah, I get it now," Brad said, "You also threw me around like 007 when we were upstairs. But what I really want to know is, why did that guy come after Adara?" Brad asked.

"He was the Idaho Shopper," Carol answered, "he stalked women in supermarkets, and Adara worked in the supermarket."

"He was after me. Somehow, he tracked me down. Inside, Gary Fletcher was a nano tech exactly like me. He originated at NeuroComm, and he knew Adara's father. He wanted to reproduce to create more hybrid humans, that's why he kidnapped those women."

"How do you know all this?" Jake asked.

"He told me."

"What? After you were knocked out?" Brad asked.

"No, we met before that. Like I said, he tracked me down and wanted me to go with him to reproduce. But I refused."

"What?" Adara screeched, "You never told me this! What if the military follows Fletcher's trail? They'll capture us and take us away!"

"I have considered that possibility, but the police think Fletcher was after you, Adara. It is unlikely that anyone will think that I am inside you, that is why we must continue to behave like a normal human."

"That's why you left us to study in college?" Brad asked.

"Yes, it was the logical choice to hide in the open. But I have other reasons to study at that college. First, I can use their facilities to explore my nano tech, who, and what I am. In addition, we can easily attain a degree and get a good job."

"And live amongst a bunch of old-fashioned age-old farts." Adara added.

"So, what happens now?" Brad asked, "What do you want us to do?"

"We continue as normal, I must remain vigilant, and none of you must ever talk about this to anyone."

"Yes, but don't even talk about this to Larry," Carol said.

"That's quite right, he could talk about this without thinking."

"Top secret mission." Jake said.

# CHAPTER 18

"You're almost as good as me in picking locks," Gina whispered.

"I had military training." As they entered the apartment, the intruder alarm started beeping a warning.

Bayu closed the front door silently behind them and entered a string of numbers on the alarm panel. The beeping immediately stopped.

"How did you know the alarm code?"

"Basically, a good guess; I used her birthdate which I got from her Facebook page."

"What if you got it wrong?"

"There are several other common codes I could have tried."

"So now that we're in this woman's apartment, what's her name again?"

"Anita Gonzalez, the secretary of NeuroComm."

"Oh, yeah, she's supposed to know everything about NeuroComm, right?"

"There is a high probability that she has much information." Bayu looked around the room, peering around corners as if searching for something.

"What are you looking for?"

"A place to install this listening device."

Bayu took off the knapsack, placing it on the couch, it reached inside, pulling out what looked like an electrical power outlet, and a screwdriver. "This is the listening device; it replaces an existing power outlet. Inside this outlet is a microphone that will record sound and conversations. It will continue to work as an ordinary electrical socket, and because it is connected to electricity, the microphone will work indefinitely. I need to decide where to place it so it can gather the best conversations."

"How about the bedroom?"

"Those conversations do not interest me."

"Have you heard the saying – you'll always find me in the kitchen at parties?"

"No, what does that mean?"

"It means the best conversations happen in the kitchen, and because this is an open-plan apartment, you can also pick up conversations from the living room and dining room."

"That is a very wise observation."

"Come on, get it right, I'm not just wise, I'm streetwise! While you're at it, install it in that socket, above the counter top, so it gets the best coverage." Gina pointed towards an electrical socket above the main kitchen worktop.

Bayu left the device and screwdriver by the socket and then went to the hallway leading to the bedroom.

"Now, where are you going?"

"I want to switch the electric power off. I do not want to have an electric shock. Also, I need to find the network gateway, there will be information on the label that will allow me to connect this microphone to it."

Bayu then turned and headed to the hallway. Opening the utility cupboard, it was filled with shoes, coats and other paraphernalia. On the top of the self was a cookie box size device standing upright connected with wires. Various lights indicated it was working and connected to the Internet, this was the home gateway, the connection to the outside world. Bayu lifted it without disturbing the wires to examine the data written on the back. The manufacturer, the serial number, and the part code were memorized immediately by Bayu. Returning it to its shelf, Bayu then opened a gray metallic utility panel on the side cupboard wall, with several switches inside. Each switch was labeled for a different electric circuit in the apartment. Bayu switched off the circuit for the kitchen sockets.

Returning to the kitchen, Bayu then used the screwdriver to open the electrical socket that Gina had suggested.

"I hope you know what you're doing."

"You say you are streetwise; well, I am technical-wise."

Bayu disconnected the electrical wires from the original socket and connected the wires to the replacement device.

"You see, this will look and act exactly like the original socket, but it also has a microphone to listen to any conversations."

"But how do we listen to those conversations?"

"This is the clever part, but wait, I have to switch the electricity back on."

Bayu screwed the device into the wall to replace the original socket. The old socket was then pocketed along with the screwdriver. Walking to the hallway cupboard, Bayu switched the circuit for the kitchen sockets back on.

Returning to the kitchen, Bayu then pulled out the laptop from their backpack and logged in.

"This device is Blue Tooth enabled, so this laptop can connect to it."

Bayu used a browser window on the laptop to log into the device. Navigating to a configuration page, Bayu entered the details of the Wi-Fi connection.

"You see, I can now connect to the home gateway with Wi-Fi, this device will send the microphone data to a cloud-based server where it will be recorded."

Bayu used the default login to connect the laptop to the household gateway. This allowed access to the internet. Logging into the cloud-based server, Bayu could then test the listening device.

"The cloud server has a ten-hour circular buffer to record any sounds."

"Only ten hours? Is that enough?"

"Yes, because it doesn't record silence, and we will be checking this every day."

They listened to the conversation they had just been having playing back over the internet on their laptop.

"That test shows it works."

"This is brilliant. You're a genius to get this working."

"This is what I and this equipment were designed for."

With the test confirmed, they packed their laptop and tools into the backpack, made sure no traces of work were left behind, and quietly departed from the apartment.

Once outside, they walked silently to the car, which was parked a block away. As they drove off, Gina asked, "So what's next? Do you have another listening device for the other person?"

"Yes, for Larisa Mandelson, the wife of the security guard, Bill Mandelson. Placing that device will be more difficult."

"Why more difficult? I saw how easily you got into that apartment."

"I will be able to access the Mandelson household just as easily, but the Mandelson family live there and I need to observe the house to determine when it will be empty."

"Sounds like a stakeout."

"Steak out? What is the relevance of food?"

"Stake out is just a saying, S-T-A-K-E, which means we have to watch the house. It's like staking a claim. Sounds like a steak to eat, but it's not."

"Is that an example of a homophone?"

"Oh, God, now I'm going to be your English teacher."

"Yes, while we wait and observe the house, you can help me improve my understanding of the language. When I determine the house is empty and safe to enter, we can install a bugging device in the kitchen."

"Well, I got to hand it to you, you are one smart cookie."

"Cookie? Yet another food reference?"

# CHAPTER 19

After strolling from the break room, Lieutenant Colonel Moore returned to his laptop, a cup of coffee in his hand. The login screen was now at last clearly displayed and waiting for input. Placing his mug to one side, he seated himself comfortably, swiveling his chair to face the keyboard. After he logged in, he reached for his mug and slurped at the hot liquid, waiting for the network connection. The vacant cubicle only offered bland, blue fabric to look at. Some distant voices discussing protein enhancements and body-building exercises revealed other marines were nearby in the office.

*Damn, these desk swap jobs, I wish I could either work from home or have my own messy desk.* He thought.

Moore's laptop slowly connected through the layers of military encryption, allowing desktop icons to activate one by one. Alerts appeared, indicating that messages were being delivered. Moore was used to this latency and used it as a meditation to prepare himself for communications. A hot mug of coffee in hand always helped.

Eventually, the email application came to life, indicating new messages. Moore glanced over, this time taking one more sip of coffee, before putting his mug to one side. Using the laptop mouse pad, he navigated through his daily sequence of emails. He eventually came to one titled '`ReportIDho-Homicide-267-F`'.

Opening the attachment, Moore realized this was the forensic report for Miss Liu's apartment. He began to read, scrolling through the pages.

All items of the apartment were listed. Furniture, crockery, clothes, shoes, sex toys, and ointments that were typical of a call girl. What became apparent was the list of bugging devices that were not typical of a call girl. Empty boxes of ammunition and traces of gunpowder.

*Hm, what was this girl up to?* Moore thought.

No laptop was recovered, suggesting the person had left, taking personal items with them. The forensic report was able to list the history of web browsing, these were obtained with the cooperation of the internet provider. Many of the websites included numerous pornography pages, but what stood out for Moore was the list of websites and documents providing instructions on how to conduct surveillance. This alone ran to many pages, with references to many downloaded documents.

*This call girl may be interested in watching or blackmailing her clients.*

Other web sites included weapons, ammunition, and most notably NeuroComm.

*This makes things even more interesting; why would she be interested in NeuroComm? Could this be the work of a spy?*

What really rattled Moore was the DNA report. Even previous residents of the apartment were listed, traced, and excluded from further investigation. One name that stood out was Professor Hayden Wolf.

*What the heck was he doing there?*

Reading further, Moore discovered that Professor Wolf's DNA was present throughout the apartment. In the kitchen, living room, bedroom, and on some sex toys.

"Holy crap!" Moore swore out loud before downloading the file to his investigation folder. *I must find out why he was there and exactly what was going on!*

When Moore finished scanning through the report, he then opened a government search for Gina Liu. When the search was complete, Moore swore again. "That's strange, her online records only go back a few years, she might as well have been born yesterday! Her full history does not exist, where the heck did she come from?"

Moore stared at the screen, thinking hard.

*Where the heck did this girl come from? Why did she suddenly appear around the same time when NeuroComm came online? Why is Wolf's DNA all over her apartment?*

Moore's brain made a connection – "Wait," he said out loud, "What about her legal protection?"

Grabbing his phone, Moore scrolled through his online case notes. "There it is." He said to himself, "The attorney for Gina Liu, Neil Lambert. That cop told me he was a military lawyer."

A quick search on the USMC database revealed Lambert's contact details. Before Moore Dialed Lambert's direct line, he emailed Lambert's superior officer and included his own office at the Pentagon.

*This should make them talk to me.* He thought.

Dialing the number, Moore waited for the connection. "Hello, this is the office of Lieutenant Lambert, how may I be of assistance?"

"I am Lieutenant Colonel Steven Moore, chief investigator on assignment from the Pentagon. I wish to speak with Neil Lambert."

"I'm sorry, but he is not available right now, may I take a message?"

"Ma'am, what is your name and rank?"

"I am Corporal Alice Reeves, USMC."

"Well, Corporal Reeves, as I said, I am on direct orders from the Pentagon. I need to speak with Lieutenant Lambert immediately. It is of the utmost importance. Please note that I have previously emailed my credentials to your office commander, and copied my commander at the Pentagon, who can confirm my orders. This information should help you validate my authority. If you need to check my credentials, please do so. In the meantime, can you please locate Lieutenant Lambert and advise him that I need to speak with him immediately."

A moment's silence before, "Please hold, I will try to connect you."

Muzak played while Moore waited to be connected to Lambert. Some minutes passed before Corporal Reeves returned to the line, "Thank you for waiting Colonel Moore, we have validated your credentials, I will connect you now."

A moment later, "This is Lieutenant Lambert, how can I be of assistance?"

"Ah, Lieutenant Lambert, my name is Lieutenant Colonel Steven Moore. I am investigating issues surrounding NeuroComm, and I would like to ask you a few questions."

"Hello Colonel, I'm not sure how I can help you. I don't have any information about this so-called NeuroComm. But what do you need to know?"

"I am looking into a civilian who has received legal protection and conveyancing support through your office."

"I'm sorry, sir, but I cannot discuss any client details without written authorization."

"Yes, I appreciate client confidentiality. I must remind you that this is not just a police matter, it is also a military investigation. I may have to remind you that it is the Pentagon that is conducting this investigation. Please take a moment to review my authorization codes that have been passed to your office. When you are satisfied, I would like you to answer my questions."

The phone line went silent for a moment. "Colonel Moore, please hold while I check through this."

This time, there wasn't any Muzak.

A few moments later, Lieutenant Lambert returned to the call. "Sir, what do you need to know?"

"Thank you for checking Lieutenant Lambert, I would expect nothing less from a Marine."

"Yes, can we get on with the questions, as I have other, more important work to do."

"Yes, we all have important work. My first question. You defended a suspect named Gina Liu on suspicion of solicitation. Is that correct?"

"Yes, that is correct, and all paperwork is in order. It is all logged in the court records for Idaho Falls."

"Who was the suspected perpetrator of this solicitation?"

"Just a moment, while I look this up." Lambert paused for a moment before answering. "It was a man named as Professor Hayden Wolf."

"Who ordered you to defend Professor Wolf?"

"It was General Bruckner."

"Were you able to vindicate Professor Wolf?"

"Yes, we were able to dismiss the case according to insufficient evidence. Professor Wolf was acquitted. Hence, Ms. Gina Liu was also acquitted."

"Thank you, Lieutenant Lambert. I have only one more question."

Moore paused before asking the next question.

"You acted as an attorney to convey the purchase of Gina Liu's apartment in Idaho Falls. Is that correct?"

"Yes, that is correct. Once again, I was operating under instruction to provide this service."

"Thank you. Who ordered you to provide this service?"

Moments later, Lambert's voice came back. "It was General Bruckner."

"Thank you, Lieutenant Lambert, you have been very helpful in my investigation."

"Is there anything else I can help you with?"

"I have no more questions, but I do have a request."

"What is it?"

"You need to forward all your records for both the solicitation court case and the conveyancing to me and to the people on copy at the Pentagon. These records need to be encrypted. Once sent, all the files you retain must be encrypted and secured as Top Secret."

"Top Secret? What the heck is going on?"

"You do not need to know what is going on. All you need to know is you must not discuss either of these cases with anyone other than myself or authorized officers from the Pentagon. Do you understand?"

"Yes, sir."

# CHAPTER 20

General George Bruckner paced the floor behind his desk. His steps were slow, but each turn was deliberate. At each end, he finished with a short step with the left foot and turned 180 degrees on the balls of both feet before continuing in the opposite direction. Head down in deep thought, he would pat the back of his office armchair with his hand as he passed behind it.

Halfway through his march, the desk phone buzzed, indicating his secretary was calling. Bruckner simply halted, shook his head, sidestepped around his chair, seating himself at his desk. He then pressed the speaker button. He answered, "Yes?"

The voice of his secretary replied, "Captain Johnson is here to see you, he is with Lieutenant Colonel Moore."

"I've been expecting them, send them in." Bruckner closed the line, then sat straight into his executive office armchair, resting his elbows on the armrests.

Captain Johnson entered the room, walking in synchronicity with Lieutenant Colonel Moore. Both held a manila folder under each left arm. Both men approached Bruckner's desk, stood to attention, and saluted, revealing no emotion. "Sir."

Bruckner returned the salute from his seated position. "So, gentlemen, what dirt have you been able to dig up for me this time?"

"Sir, we have good news and bad news," Johnson said as he completed his salute.

"Take a seat and please keep the clichés out."

Both Johnson and Moore both sat in front of Bruckner's desk, and Johnson retrieved the printed report from his folder, offering it to Bruckner.

Bruckner glanced at it but remained still. Ignoring the folder, he simply asked. "Well, Johnson, what do you and Moore have to tell me?"

"Sir, I think it is best that the Colonel outlines this report for you."

"Well, Colonel, my captain says you should outline this report."

"Yes, sir." Moore leaned forward as he opened the report on his lap. "I can start with the Pentagon, confirming that Fletcher had nanobots in his blood."

Bruckner interrupted. "Why are they repeating that? They stated that in the last report." Bruckner now reached out, indicating that Johnson's hands the report to him. "Let me have a look at this!"

"Well, sir, I think they are just reinforcing the fact. You know how reports are, there's always a lot of cut and paste."

"Have they examined the contents of the vials that were in the fire?"

"Yes, sir, that's also repeated in this report. All they say is the contents were a cooked soup of biological material. They have a list of the suspected components after spectral analysis."

"Can they rebuild the nano cells?"

"If anything, sir, their current answer is a negative, but I would guess they are working on options."

Bruckner sat back in frustration. "This is getting like a ten-question game, is there anything new?"

"Sir, it is all in the report."

"Does it mention the software?"

Moore nodded. "Yes, sir, it mentions the software, but it has been lost in the fire. All the hard drives were destroyed, making them unreadable, or they had been wiped. The Pentagon suspects they were all wiped prior to the fire, which suggests deliberate sabotage."

"Sabotage?" Bruckner looked quizzical.

"Yes," Johnson replied, "this is the first time they are using that term, and they seem to use it in earnest."

"What do you mean, in earnest?"

"Well, sir," Moore continued, "the Pentagon suspects that sabotage was the cause of the fire. In particular, the report points to a possible rift between Professor Wolf and Dr. Coney. The report suggests that it is more likely that Coney was acting as the saboteur, as he had thorough knowledge of the local lab network and how to wipe the hard drives."

"Why would they suspect Coney?"

"According to their records, Doctor Coney had a small but inconsequential history of social, well how should I say this, social critique?"

"Was he a rebel?"

"Not exactly, sir. He was outspoken in his college days, and he had some frictional encounters with previous employers. He seems to have moved on from these without any serious trouble."

"So, he had a confrontation with Wolf?"

"That is a possibility, sir. He may have had a serious confrontation with Professor Wolf."

"So that may have explained the fire?"

Colonel Moore wavered at the answer. "Sir, the report seems to fall short of that conclusion, but it has been left as a distinct possibility. For instance, they say the fire was started at various strategic locations, indicating deliberate malice. I think they fall short of accusing any person as they do not yet have a motive."

"I see."

"There are also questions raised in the report about Professor Wolf, many of these relate to operational issues."

"Operational issues?"

"Yes, sir, there are several, but the most important questions are as follows,"

Moore now started to list them on his fingers.

"The first question addresses software backup. Why wasn't a better backup regime implemented? They state that software should have been backed up off-site, on a military backup server."

Moore paused, "Do you know if any backups were made? Is there any off-site backup of data?"

"I didn't discuss issues like that with Professor Wolf, I assumed he had everything under control."

"Second, why weren't any of the nanotech vials backed up off-site?"

"Again, all I can say is, I assumed Wolf had this under control. Very few of these vials were made, maybe the professor wanted them all under his control. Who knows, perhaps he was also worried about keeping his creation to himself. If he released it to the military, he probably thought his work would be abandoned. Isn't this a common feeling with startups?"

"Hm, that's a fair point." Moore scribbled a note on his copy of the report. When he finished, he raised his head, looking towards Bruckner. "Another question they raise in this report is the size of the nanotech vials."

"The size?" Bruckner shrugged.

"Yes, sir, the vials used for animals such as birds and dogs were not just empty, they were stored as if they would not be needed again."

Bruckner's glance moved between Moore and Johnson, both of whom simply stared straight back.

Moore continued, "The size and scope of the remaining vials were radically different, suggesting they were intended for an animal the size and weight of a human."

"Ah, back to the human experiment." Bruckner nodded. "Like I said, I knew nothing of this, and how am I supposed to know about vial sizes used in their experiments?"

"Well, sir, the report references another document on operational practices that states details such as this must be listed and recorded."

"Details such as what?" Bruckner demanded.

Moore leaned back in his chair and took a deep breath. "Did you list any of these operational changes such as vial size?"

"Wait!" Bruckner thumbed through the report on his desk. "Is this report trying to pin the blame on me?" Looking up, he scowled at Moore. "Are you looking to make me the scapegoat?"

"No, sir."

"Then why all these accusations?"

"These aren't accusations, sir, I have simply fed my investigations back to the Pentagon. They obviously have questions raised by their level of analysis."

Moore paused on the word analysis. "I'm just letting you know these questions will eventually be left for you, sir, to answer."

Bruckner slammed the report back on his desk and rested back in his chair, raising his eyes to the ceiling. "Uh, jeez, this is crazy." He mumbled.

"Sir," Captain Johnson interrupted, "Moore is only stating the contents of the Pentagon report."

"Yes, sir," Moore continued, "All I'm handing you is the Pentagon's report."

"Damn it Moore! What I want to know is, aside from their questions, can they recover any nanobots and restart the research?"

"Not exactly, sir. If you look at page thirty-seven, the labs conclude that any samples they obtained were too decomposed to determine any physical details of the nanobots. All they could say was the nanobot cells were of a biomechanical nature, they could not discover any means of how they work."

Bruckner's eyes widened as he thumbed to page thirty-seven, his fingers trembling slightly. "What about Fletcher's body? Is there anything that could be recovered from that?"

"Negative, sir. This is also their conclusion of the lab remains and the blood samples from Fletcher's body. The estranged family had his body cremated at their earliest convenience. I suspect they wanted to distance themselves from what he did."

Bruckner shook his head as he looked through the report.

Moore continued, "Sir, the samples in Fletcher's body mean we have formal confirmation that Fletcher was a hybrid. A human experiment has been confirmed to be underway. The question remains, was this experiment authorized? And if so, who allowed it?"

Bruckner looked up, "Authorized? What are you suggesting?"

Moore kept his gaze on Bruckner. "Originally, the Pentagon wanted to know where the three missing nanotech vials are. Now that the labs have confirmed a hybrid human, that will account for one of those vials. Leaving two vials still missing. But the Pentagon wants to know who authorized this experiment."

Bruckner broke his gaze with Moore, looking down at the report, he said, "We already knew that fingerprints and DNA confirmed both Mandelson &

Wolf were at the safe house. They must have been acting alone."

"The question is, why would they be acting at all?" Moore asked.

"They were acting alone!" Bruckner insisted. "What else is in this report?"

Johnson interrupted again. "As we mentioned, it seems that Dr. Coney became aware of the human experiment and tried to put a stop to the project. This is probably the cause of the fire and the destruction of the lab."

Bruckner shook his head and mumbled expletives under his breath. After a moment, he spoke out. "What about Fletcher's victims, is there any connection with them? Maybe Fletcher was eliminating contacts."

Moore answered. "I have a subordinate who is making the relevant inquiries. He will find out if there are any links with them and the military. So far, he has not identified any connection."

"What about the motive?" Bruckner locked his gaze directly at Moore. "Have you been able to determine why Fletcher did what he did?"

"Sir, the only explanation is insanity. This technology was unproven as a human enhancement. The fact that Fletcher had a history of drug abuse and mental instability could not have helped."

"What about the official line on Fletcher?" Bruckner asked.

"Fletcher was a serial killer, which is reflected by his dubious background," Moore said. "The official story stands in the public eye."

"But the Pentagon considers this a serious crime," Johnson added.

Bruckner sighed, "Gentlemen, is there anything else I need to be aware of?"

Moore looked at Johnson and waited.

"There's an entire section in that report on Gina Liu, which Moore has been investigating. I'll let him brief you on that." Johnson then turned to Moore.

"Thank you, Captain." Colonel Moore deftly opened his folder, retrieving his secondary report. Keeping his eyes on the paperwork, he moved to hand it over the desk to Bruckner. As he did so, Moore raised his eyes to engage Bruckner's, "This is my report on the suspect, Gina Liu."

Both men relaxed into their chairs. Moore opened his copy of his report to a specific page.

"Please turn to page nine," Moore said. "This section confirms the relationship between Gina Liu and Rodrigo Carlos Fernando, commonly known as Rocco."

"Rocco?" Bruckner asked.

"Rodrigo Carlos Fernando," Moore replied, "A known minor criminal suspected of acting as a pimp. My agent and I have interviewed several women who have corroborated the connection between Gina Liu and Rodrigo Carlos Fernando. These women prefer to be known as escorts."

"You mean prostitutes?" Bruckner scoffed.

"No, I do not mean prostitutes," Moore held his gaze, with a condescending smirk, "I mean working women. The definition here is irrelevant, the important point is the connection between Mr. Fernando and Miss Liu. All the girls who agreed to be questioned reported that Gina was a kind and caring person, she also acted as their interface to Rocco, she was the 'madam' who was looking after them."

"Why do I need to know this detail?"

"Look further on page eleven. You will see that Gina Liu's identity is false. Her identity and social security number were adopted from a long-since deceased person. The original identity is listed in appendix 2."

"She was using a false name and identity? What are you implying?"

"What this tells me is that Gina Liu is not who she said she was, she is of unidentifiable origin. This is common in escort girls; it is natural for women in this industry to hide their true identity. But Gina's is particularly interesting. Working girls often want to be held as anonymous for their own personal reasons. However, all searches for Ms. Liu's genuine history have led to a blank, it seems that several years ago she simply did not exist."

"Oh, my God!"

Moore flicked a few pages forward. "Now turn to pages sixteen and seventeen, where we have listings of the apartment contents. The list includes many items, such as model XQJ-37 electrically powered eavesdropping device. This, along with other surveillance equipment, suggests that she is a spy."

"What?"

"Yes, I suspect she is a Chinese sleeper agent who has infiltrated this project.

Bruckner coughed, "What? But how?"

"According to the call girls we interviewed, they stated that Gina Liu has been away from the call girl work for over one year. This matches the time when the project was becoming known. Rocco may have suspected something and tried to confront her, which explains his brutal murder."

Moore looked up at Bruckner, whose hand was beginning to tremble. "Let's continue to the open questions about finance, which begin on page eighteen."

All men lowered their heads, looking back to the report.

"There are various funds which are attached to the Fletcher case, not least of which is a house and property valued at $300,000 near Spencer, Idaho. This house is a safe house, north of Idaho Falls, where Fletcher was based. These funds and assets are currently being reclaimed by our legal team."

Bruckner looked at the figures.

Moore continued. "Sir, the following page outlines the missing funds which are likely to be connected to Gina Liu."

Moore kept his eyes on Bruckner before continuing. "I forgot to mention that in the section outlining the contents of the apartment contents, the forensic team also found fingerprints and DNA from Professor Wolf. The question is, why was he there?

Obviously, Wolf spent some time there with Ms. Liu. Are you able to explain this?"

"How should I know what Wolf was doing?"

"Well, as the General overseeing this project, I would have thought you would have kept a closer watch on the finances and paid closer attention to the project members."

"What the heck are you insinuating?" demanded Bruckner.

"I'm not insinuating anything; all I am doing is investigating the facts."

"Well, what does your investigation tell us?"

"There may have been blackmail involved."

"Blackmail? What the heck?"

"Yes, I think it's plain as day. Gina Liu is a sleeper agent acting as a call girl within earshot of Idaho National Laboratory. INL is a hive of cutting-edge development, it is still home to some of our atomic energy development, but the campus is also home to many high-tech startup companies. Never mind the nuclear secrets, any intellectual property developed there could be invaluable to the Chinese industry."

Moore let that sink in.

"She is probably there trying to get leverage into the nuclear research. Somehow, she gets wind of NeuroComm, a new and secretive startup company, connected to the military with the potential for human enhancement." Moore shrugged his shoulders, "Possibly, her bosses in Beijing alerted her after they heard some noise on the wires about NeuroComm. But one way or another, this project became her target.

Normally, a talented engineer of Chinese origin would get a job to steal the company's secrets, but this isn't high-class Silicon Valley. This is working-class Idaho, and working as a call girl, it was probably easy for her to seduce Wolf. He is married, with children, and he has a reputation to maintain. Once he fell into her trap, it was probably very easy for her to drag him down her rabbit hole. If you'll pardon the pun."

"That's incredible."

"It probably didn't end with money, that was probably just the bait. Her target was to get access to the technology."

"What do you mean?"

"It is quite possible that she used her sexual leverage to get hold of the missing nanotech vials. That would be the crown jewels for her."

Bruckner gasped. "So, what next?"

"It's obvious," Moore stated, "we need to get hold of Gina Liu. The Canadian border is closest, but we have that securely covered. We've also alerted the Canadian authorities. We've alerted every port and airport in the country to apprehend her on-sight. It's only a matter of time before we get her."

"Jeezus, will we get the missing nanotech back?"

"Sir, I do not have a crystal ball." Moore stood up, placing his copy of the report back in his folder. "All I can say, sir, is every person involved in this project will be closely audited. Now, if you will excuse me, I have a prime suspect to apprehend."

With that, Moore left the meeting.

# CHAPTER 21

Being a marine, Tom Vance was used to orders and always followed them to the letter. Orders would come in many forms, verbal, written, or through radio comms. Following the orders exactly would usually require some personal interpretation, after all, marines are trained to think around the dynamics of any situation.

He would always look after the men in his charge, it wasn't just a case of 'no man gets left behind', he would carefully explain the mission parameters, making sure every soldier understood the rules of engagement and the avenues of escape. The Marines always work as a team. But if a marine gets separated, then we must think out of the box. Returning to our rendezvous point as best we can.

This mission was different, he was used to working alone in the field, but in this case there were no dynamic situations. Interviewing suspects, mostly call girls, collating their statements and reporting the information back to Moore. Vance only met occasionally with Colonel Moore, all the leads and orders he received came through the phone. Tom called it the 'Yakety Yak App' because it always informed him of useless information. Mostly it was text messages, but if Moore called on this app, then the phone would continuously retry until he answered it.

*I suspect it's got geo-location, so I can't even take a crap in private.*

Tom was driving when the phone started ringing again, it could only be Moore, and it must be important. Tom had just finished an interview with a call girl, all the data was uploaded. *Hm, I wonder if Moore found some sort of connection with this girl?*

Holding the steering wheel with one hand, he answered. "Yes, sir, this is Tom."

"Colonel Moore here, I have some important updates for you."

"Yes, sir. Do you have more leads?"

"I have a new priority for you, her name is Gina Liu."

"Have you located her?"

"That's the trouble, we suspect she is on the run. As we speak, I am uploading all the data we have on her, as well as some photos taken from the supermarket video."

As Moore said that, the phone beeped intermittently, showing that files were being received.

"Included in these files is the forensic report on her apartment. You will see from the evidence that she is a spy, probably for the Chinese government. We also believe that she is in possession of one or both missing nanotech vials."

"Any idea where she is?"

"That's the trouble, we don't know. I suspect she's heading for an extraction point; that's the only sensible option for her."

"Canada is the closest border," Tom suggested.

"I've already thought of that, both the Canadian and Mexican borders have been alerted, along with airports. I think she's too smart to try those routes, she'll need help to get out of this country. She must be heading for an extraction point which will smuggle her and the nanotech back to China."

"The biggest Chinese communities I know are Los Angeles and San Francisco."

"Exactly."

"Do you want me to head down there? Do you have any leads for me to investigate?"

"We already have coverage on those communities, the NSA is on alert and listening to the comms down there. So, I don't have any new leads yet, I need you to stay put and sniff out any clues to where she may be heading, maybe there's something in the interviews you took. Did any of those girls mention any friends of hers?"

"NSA? Holy crap! This is really heating up!"

"As I said before, this is the utmost national security. We cannot, and I repeat, we cannot allow this technology to fall into foreign hands."

"What about her car, do you know if she's driving?"

"We have the make of her car; the details are included in the files I sent you. So far, this hasn't been located. We don't know if she's already left in that car or if she's dumped it. Every highway patrol has been alerted between here and all surrounding states, including California. If she's using that car, we'll find her."

"Well, if she's as smart as you say, she's dumped it."

"One last thing. If you encounter her, alert us first and approach with caution. She is highly dangerous and armed."

"I have my sidearm."

"Yeah, so did that Rocco guy. I have to go; the Pentagon wants a status update. Moore out."

The line went dead as Moore hung up.

Tom dumped the phone into an empty drinks holder and quickly pulled over into a supermarket parking lot. *Jeezus, how the hell am I supposed to find clues to Liu's whereabouts? Guess I'm going to start over from the beginning, see if I missed anything.*

# CHAPTER 22

Gina pointed to the left, "Pull over into that parking lot."

"Why?"

"I want a cup of coffee," she said, "that's why."

"Coffee is a waste of our resources. We've already had breakfast."

"As usual, I didn't sleep well, so right now, a good cup of coffee is an excellent investment in my resources."

Bayu pulled into the parking lot and stopped a row away from Starbucks. "OK, we just get a small coffee and get straight back in the car."

"No way, I want to sit in there, stretch my legs, and act like a human, you can wait in the car if you want."

"What?"

"I'm kidding, but I want some time off to sit comfortably in there." Gina opened the car door, "Switch the phone on and bring it with us. We can use the earphones to check your cloud recordings while we're there."

"Remember, we must not talk to each other when we're in there."

“How about if I text myself? Would that make us happy?”

Gina walked into Starbucks and smiled as the staff greeted her. There was the usual chatter, a man sat at a table tapping into his laptop. Some ladies were sharing a cake at another table whilst gossiping with each other. While Gina waited in line, she looked at the notice on the wall so Bayu could see. A sign displayed the Wi-Fi password. She whispered, “There is Wi-Fi here.”

The woman in front of Gina half turned, but before she could look at Gina.

“Next in line,” the server announced.

Stepping forward, the woman ordered her latte and a sweet bun. As they waited, Bayu logged into the cloud server but kept constant watch on their environment.

When it became Gina’s turn, she ordered a pumpkin spice latte with a banana bread slice.

“`Never mind the banana bread,`” Bayu said.

“I like banana bread, and it goes well with the pumpkin latte.”

“Um, mam? Do you want the banana bread or not?”

“`Never mind the banana bread,`” Bayu repeated.

“I guess it has too many calories.” Gina said, “Just the Pumpkin spice latte, it’s seasonal, and it’s been so long since I had one.”

“Absolutely mam, coming right up.”

Gina paid with cash and waited to one side for her latte. Bayu accessed the recordings from the Mandelson home while Gina watched the screen. Each recording had a time stamp, they listened to them and all they could hear was kitchen cooking noises and kids arguing.

“Kitchen noise and kids arguing,” Gina said out loud. Realizing that other customers were looking at her, she held up the phone and said, “Sorry”.

Bayu deleted the unwanted recordings.

“Pumpkin Spice Latte for Gina,”

“Hey, that’s me! Thanks!” Picking up the Pumpkin Spice Latte in one hand, and the iPhone in the other, Gina walked over towards an empty table by the window. As they went, Bayu used one eye to view the iPhone screen.

“God, that makes me dizzy!” Gina hissed under her breath.

Bayu then switched to the App, monitoring Anita’s apartment, silently showing with her thumb to Gina that the current recording was live. They listened to the conversation on the earphones and realized Anita was talking with a man about NeuroComm.

“Whoa!” Gina exclaimed out loud, “We have to go!”

Everyone in the room turned towards Gina, except for the man with the laptop, who continued to stare at his screen.

“`What do you mean?`” Bayu asked.

"We must find out who that guy is! The way they are talking, he sounds important!" Gina had placed her coffee on the table, only to grab it again. Getting up to go, she continued, "We have to get there before he leaves!"

"You're right, this could be an important connection," Bayu said.

All eyes followed Gina out of the coffee shop. As Gina jumped in the car, she asked, "Do you remember how to get there?"

"Of course I do. I have the whole city map memorized."

---

Gina had just placed her cardboard cup of Pumpkin Spice Latte safely in the drink holder when Bayu drove the Prius into the street. Turning right to head towards the apartment complex where Anita Gonzalez lived. Although accelerating fast, Bayu kept to the speed limit, not wanting to attract the attention of any police.

"Did you hear what he just said?" Gina asked, "He's talking about Bill Mandelson as if he was an old friend."

"Yes, and I'm concerned that you talked too much in that coffee shop."

"Well, you were talking too!"

"Only because you were, you know how dangerous that can be for us."

"I can't believe I'm arguing with a robot! Oh, wait, yes, I can, because that robot lives inside my body! What else can be this crazy in my life? Anyway, can we please be quiet so I can listen to their conversation?"

"I am listening to their conversation, I can multitask. I can drive, listen to the conversation, and argue with you at the same time."

"Well, I can't!"

"Don't worry, the conversation is being recorded so we can replay it."

"What's his name?"

"I don't know yet; it may have been mentioned earlier before we started listening."

The conversation streaming through the iPhone seemed to be coming to an end.

"Are we there yet?" Gina asked.

They then heard the woman say, "Thank you, Lieutenant Vance, please keep me informed, and stay away from those military police."

"Bingo!" Gina exclaimed, "That's his name, Mr. Vance."

"Correction, his name is Lieutenant Vance, which means he is in the military."

At that moment, Bayu signaled to turn left into the apartment parking lot. Selecting a parking space near Anita's flat, Bayu pulled into it to face a blank fence.

"That was dumb, has your calculator blown a fuse? You should have reversed into this spot so we could keep a good watch on the doorway."

Bayu adjusted the rear-view mirror and the side mirrors. "I have eyes everywhere; I can see what I need to see."

Moments later, two men emerged from the doorway, both dressed in smart, casual clothes.

"I only heard one male voice through the iPhone, so I don't think they are together. Which one is our Mr. Vance?"

Bayu started calculating probabilities. "One looks mature, average weight, and healthy. The second is middle-aged, fit, healthy, and much more muscular. The first one is about five foot ten inches with graying hair, the second man is approximately six feet with slightly dark hair. I calculate a 40/60 percent probability of that the second man is the correct person to follow."

"I disagree. Follow my lead on this one, there is no 50/50 on this. Our target is the man with the dark hair, he is our Mr. Vance."

"How can you be so sure?"

"Easy, from the voice on the recording. It was a younger middle aged man, not an older person. Also, if he was a friend of Bill Mandelson, then he must be a contemporary of a similar age."

"OK, I concur with your logic, we will follow him."

The older man got into a small compact car, slightly out of view of their mirrors.

The younger man walked further to his car, and Gina had to look through the windows of several parked cars to see where he went.

“He's getting into a large white pickup truck.”

“What make?”

“I do not know.”

As the pickup pulled out and drove behind Gina towards the street, Gina said, “Start the engine and follow him, he's driving a RAM.”

“I have his license plate number.”

“Good, follow at a safe distance.”

“I know how to follow suspects. Professor Wolf gave me a rating of 96% on my pursuit tests.”

“So, you are 4% off perfect. Don't worry, sweetheart, I'll tell you when you need to slow down and keep your distance.”

Bayu kept both eyes on the target car ahead and maintained a safe distance.

---

“Can you keep your eyes on the road and stop looking at the phone with one eye?”

“I want to replay that conversation while we follow Mr. Vance.”

Bayu thumbed the app, selecting the most recent recording to play. Listening to the recording through ear plugs, they heard Anita talking to a man.

"This is just small talk. Can we skip forward a bit?"

Bayu used the thirty-second skip button to jump to the next part of the conversation.

"Keep going."

After a few more skips, Bayu stopped, listening to the playback. "`Did you hear that? Anita mentioned the military.`" Bayu then rewound and played the following section of the conversation.

"So, you are now part of this military investigation?" Anita asked.

"Yes, that's right." Vance replied, "I think they pulled me in because I was a friend of William Mandelson. I guess they think I can have an advantage in finding out what happened."

"This is not good," Anita said, "are you questioning me now? I already have been questioned a lot by the military investigators."

"Of course not, I had no choice but to join the investigation. My priority is to find out what happened to my friend William, if I can help find the missing nanotech, then that's a bonus, but I think the two missing vials are long gone."

"So, two missing vials?" Anita asked. "Nobody has found them yet?"

"The military thinks they have either been stolen or sold to a Chinese agent." There was a pause before Vance continued talking. "Have you seen this woman at NeuroComm? Her name is Gina Liu."

"Jeezus, that's me!" Gina exclaimed.

"I have never seen this woman, she has never been to NeuroComm." Anita said, "Who is she?"

"Her name is Gina Liu, she's a suspected Chinese agent, we think she has the missing nanotech. She is also the suspect who killed Rodrigo Carlos Fernando."

"The killing was on the news," Anita said. "But nothing about China."

"Yes, Fernando was a pimp known as Rocco. I interviewed his call girls, at first, they didn't want to talk to the police, but they eventually admitted to knowing Liu, and confirmed she worked for Rocco. They also said that Liu was a nice girl, they didn't believe she killed Rocco."

"Maybe she didn't kill him," Anita said.

"We don't know for sure until we question her. The military thinks she fits the profile of an agent, kind to everyone she meets, but inside, she's a deadly trained killer."

"Well, he got that right!" Gina said, "Inside me is a deadly trained killer. I wonder what happens if they catch me and put me in jail, but you're the guilty culprit?"

"Silence, let's listen."

"Was Mandelson involved with her?" Anita asked.

"We have no evidence of that. But Professor Wolf's DNA and fingerprints are all over Liu's apartment. We need to understand the collusion between Wolf and Liu. Needless to say, this doesn't look good on the military oversight for this project. This mess has gone up to the Pentagon and beyond. Heads will roll, and I think General Bruckner is already on the chopping block."

"Will I be in trouble? I was working at NeuroComm."

"No, they've done background checks and what connections you had with the inner workings at NeuroComm. They say you are not a suspect."

"Thank God, but I am still so frightened. What about your friend, Bill Mandelson?"

"Well, he died in the fire, all the witnesses say he was trying to save Wolf and Coney. We can't ask him any questions, but there's no evidence to suggest he was involved with Liu, the Chinese agent. But he was involved with Gary Fletcher."

"Fletcher? The supermarket killer?"

"Fletcher has been confirmed to have been injected with the nanotech. All the evidence suggests that Bill was helping Professor Wolf run an unauthorized human trial, with Gary Fletcher as the subject."

Anita gasped, "Oh my God, were they all part of the serial killings?"

"No, that started after the fire at NeuroComm, where Bill and Wolf both died. We think Fletcher went crazy with the nanotech inside him. He was left alone with no one to help him."

"There is one thing I wanted to ask you, Anita."

"What is it?"

"Have you told anyone about Bill's trips to Twin Falls?"

"Of course not, the military has no business to know about Bill's affair. If they knew, they would question his poor wife Larisa, and that would break her heart. That poor woman has been through enough already."

"He was having more than an affair."

"What? What do you mean by that?"

"He had a wife and child in Twin Falls."

Gina blinked as she perceived the pause of astonishment between Anita and Mr. Vance.

"What?" Anita eventually asked, "How could he do that to Larisa?"

"I don't know, but it has been going on for a long time, his daughter in Twin Falls is now grown up."

"How do you know this?"

"When Bill died, I had to deliver a life insurance document to his other wife, Beryl Banks. She thought that Bill was in the special forces and died while fighting overseas. He used the name William Banks when he was with Beryl."

"This is crazy, does this Beryl Banks know about Larisa?"

"No, she doesn't know anything about Bill's real life. Although which of Bill's lives was real, I do not know."

"You said that Beryl Banks has a daughter?"

"Yes, her name is Adara Banks."

"And you met them?"

"Yes, I met both his other wife, Beryl and his daughter Adara, when I delivered Bill's insurance."

"Well, at least he took care of them with that insurance."

"Yes, Larisa and the boys also received insurance payouts, so they also are comfortable."

"Have you told Larisa about this Beryl woman and her daughter?"

"Of course, not. I have told no one, and you need to keep this secret as well. I'm going to visit Larisa next; I'm having lunch with her and the boys."

"I think I've heard enough." Bayu kept an eye on the pickup truck a few cars ahead of them. "We're almost at the Mandelson house, since we know where he's going, we don't need to follow him anymore."

Bayu then turned right into the next street.

"So, this Mandelson guy has been leading a double life as a bigamist," Gina said.

“As that Mr. Vance said, he was having more than an affair.”

“That’s for sure!”

Bayu stopped at the side of a quiet residential street. “Don’t you see the connection? He had a daughter called Adara.”

“Yeah, he was a bigamist with another family.”

“Adara Banks, of Twin Falls, was the last victim of Fletcher, she’s also the only one who survived.”

“Why would Fletcher go all that way to find a victim in Twin Falls?”

“Exactly!” Bayu opened Google on the phone. “We have to go there to find out why. First, we need the address of this Beryl Banks.” Typing the name and a few keywords, the phone number and address were soon returned. “Next we need some background on this Adara Banks!” What came up at the top of the search was an old newspaper article about Adara Banks being in a coma after a white-water accident. Bayu paged through several articles faster than Gina could read them.

“You, see? Adara Banks suffered a drowning accident while white-water rafting with her father William Banks.”

“AKA Bill Mandelson.”

“Adara makes a miraculous recovery, but her father disappears and is not available for comment. Her mother believes that it's God’s intervention.”

"Something fishy went on there."

"Fletcher is the first missing nanotech, I am the second, and I think I just found the third!"

"Holy crap, that professor trained you well as a spy."

"Yes, let's go, we need to meet this Adara Banks!"

# CHAPTER 23

*It's a chilly southern breeze,* Tom thought as he stepped out onto the porch, *the gathering clouds probably mean rain is on its way.*

Larisa Mandelson followed him out and stood outside the front door.

Tom turned to face her, "Thanks for a lovely afternoon."

"It was our pleasure," Larisa replied, "the boys always love to see you. They love listening to your stories about you and Bill. Today was the first time they laughed since we lost him."

"I'm glad I could help."

"You said you have to go back on duty, is it anything dangerous?"

Tom shook his head, "Oh, no, nothing like that, it's an investigation into a murder, that's all."

Larisa looked quizzical, "Since when are you a detective?"

"Since they transferred me to this unit. There is a case they put me on that I can't talk about," Tom looked away for a moment, "but there's another case which involves the murder of a pimp which I feel in my guts is connected."

"You don't mean that Rocco case that happened downtown the other day. It was in the news."

Tom looked up at the cloudy sky and smirked, "I can neither confirm nor deny."

Larisa scoffed, "Well, I don't need to know about those shenanigans and keep those stories away from my boys. They have enough stress with Bill gone."

"Don't worry," Tom smiled, "this has nothing to do with you and the kids." Turning to leave, he continued, "Anyway, I have to go, I got some bad guys to catch, but I'll keep in touch. Like I said, I'll take the boys to the zoo as soon as I have some time."

Larisa touched Tom's shoulder, pulling him around to face her, she then leaned forward to give him a gentle kiss on his cheek. "By the way, that insurance thing about William Banks in Twin Falls, did you ever sort that out?"

Tom took an uncertain step back, as if to move off the porch. "Um, yes, that's all taken care of, you don't need to worry about that."

"I'm so glad, one thing less to worry about."

Tom nodded, "Yes, one less thing." Turning away, he walked off the porch to the sidewalk. "See you later."

Waving over his shoulder, he thought to himself, *Next stop has to be Beryl and Adara Banks. There's something missing down there, and it's not just Bill's bigamy. I need to find out what really happened there.* Getting into his truck he paused, *First, I need a good night's sleep before that long drive, I can be in Twin Falls tomorrow, mid-morning.*

Walking away from the house, he passed a line of parked cars. Inside one of the cars, a Toyota Prius, a female Asian driver, sat still behind the steering wheel. She had earplugs, probably listening to music.

Strangely, her head was turned away towards the street, but Tom could almost swear, her eyes were turned directly towards him as he walked past.

Bayu waited until Tom got into his car before starting the engine. As Tom pulled into the street and moved away, Bayu followed behind at a safe distance.

"So, you think he's worth following and giving up on Mrs. Mandelson?" Gina asked.

"Definitely." Bayu said, "You heard what was said during their lunch, and you heard what he said that he's investigating Rocco's murder. He's on top of this case and we need to follow him. We still have the listening device in Mrs. Mandelson's kitchen, so we can keep track of her through the recordings on the cloud."

"I wonder what the other case he's working on is, and why would he think they are connected?"

Bayu didn't reply immediately as it was focusing on maintaining a safe distance from Tom's car. At the same time, Bayu was running a statistical calculation. Finally, it replied, "There is a probability that the other case is the NeuroComm investigation."

"How do you work that out?"

"He is a USMC Lieutenant , acting as an investigator, he also knows Bill Mandelson. Those two points alone suggest he is investigating NeuroComm."

"And if he thinks the Rocco murder is connected…"

"It will be only a matter of time before he starts looking for us."

Gina giggled.

"What's so funny?"

"Robots don't see the funny side of things, but we are following him!"

# CHAPTER 24

A cold damp morning, in pre-dawn darkness. Lieutenant Thomas Vance loaded his pickup truck and contemplated the drive ahead.

*Jeez. It is a two-and-a-half-hour drive.* He thought to himself.

*This is the last connection to Gary Fletcher, whom Lieutenant* Colonel *Moore wants me to interview.* Tom thought. *The girl, Adara Banks, is the only one to survive Fletcher's kidnap attempt.*

Tom adjusted his rear-view mirror and mentally reviewed his checklist. Tom wasn't worried about the overnight bag or his toothbrush. The GPS was only for the last mile to help locate the address. He did this trip once before, so he knew the route. His chief concern was his weapons and ammunition.

His personal Glock 19M, Sidearm with safety on, tucked comfortably in the driver-side door pocket. Check. *Ah, my old pal Jim, what a bond we have together.* Tom reached into the side door pocket to reassuringly touch his side arm.

Tom's Glock was a standard USMC issue and was compact enough to manage as a concealed carry. The other weapon was an M4A1 Carbine. Again, standard USMC kit, but this was issued by Lieutenant Colonel Moore. According to Moore, it could be needed in emergencies. Tom could not imagine what sort of emergency could arise while interviewing contacts. He kept this rifle in its case in a lockbox in the back, along with ammunition.

Once he was satisfied that his kit was complete, he started the engine and reversed his truck onto the road. It was still early morning, so heading towards Highway 15 was easy, as most lights stayed green. Following the signs to the highway, Tom took the slip road that headed east towards Twin Falls. Only a few early commuters were on the highway, so accelerating up to a reasonable speed, he pressed his back into the driving seat, trying to relax into a comfortable cruising posture.

*It's no use*, he thought, *I will not enjoy this part of the investigation. The others were more like interviews, this one, I don't know how to handle.*

Tom fidgeted before switching the radio on, turning to the local chart pop station. The commercials irritated him more, surfing through channels, he only found what he thought to be tedious music. *It's all crap*. He thought before switching the radio off.

Traveling west, darkness lay in the rear-view mirror, while the feint glow of dawn beckoned him forward.

"That's what I need," Tom said out loud, "head towards the light." *That was a catchphrase from an old movie*, he thought, *something about ghosts. Maybe that's why I feel so spooked about this meeting. In fact, this whole case stinks. Human enhancement technology, rogue human experiments, not to mention, a kidnapping serial killer.*

In frustration, Tom switched the radio back on and surfed through a few channels. Avoiding the current affairs channels, he paused only on the music. When he caught a song he liked, it was at the tail end, which only frustrated him more. After a few loops around the FM spectrum, he switched the radio off again.

Tom approached an area of ancient lava beds, formed thousands of years ago. Rugged rocks and sparse vegetation. The sky ahead was filled with red clouds of pre-dawn light, spreading an eerie glow across the rocky landscape.

*This certainly looks like hell's half-acre now. What's that old saying? Red sky in the morning, sailors take warning. Ghosts and warnings of shipwrecks are all I need, whatever next?*

*I'm heading into a hellish triangle, which I have to figure out. There's Gary Fletcher, the human experiment that went rogue. My old friend Bill Mandelson, who we have plenty of forensic evidence to show that he was Fletcher's handler. Then there's Adara Banks, whom Fletcher tried to kidnap. That leaves me with the three points of the triangle, but it's the connections that I can't figure out.*

Tom's eyes were focused on the highway ahead as he sped towards the dawn's early light. His mouth sometimes grimaced, suggesting the struggle he had working out his problem.

"So, Fletcher and Bill are proven to be connected," Tom said out loud. *I know that Beryl Banks and William Banks were married. I was able to check their records online. I even know that Adara Banks is their child, as I accessed her birth certificate. So, my old friend Bill Mandelson was moonlighting as William Banks in another bigamist marriage. Since there is no death certificate of William Banks, this sort of proves that fact.*

Tom sat quietly for a moment before tightening his grip on the steering wheel. "Why the heck would

Fletcher go all the way to Twin Falls to kidnap Adara?" *This is the real question I have to figure out.* He thought to himself. *The official belief is that Adara is just another victim in Fletcher's killing spree. No one else knows that Bill was a bigamist and Adara was his other daughter.*

"That's the thing." He said out loud again. *I must figure out why Fletcher went to Twin Falls. But how do I even find out? What am I supposed to ask? Hey Adara, why did Gary Fletcher try to kidnap you?*

"Jeez!" he said, shaking his head.

*What do they call that strategy of inquiry? Inferring the facts through indirect questions? I guess that's how I must play this. They probably don't even know why they would know anything about Fletcher, but that still leaves my unanswered question. Why did Fletcher go to Twin Falls?*

Tom passed a large tractor trailer, as he pulled in front of the truck, he sped off ahead.

*There is no reason for Bill to discuss his private life with Fletcher. He may have overheard Bill talking about his wife Larisa, but there is no way that Bill would have talked to anyone about his bigamy. So how could Fletcher make any connection? This is too much of a coincidence.*

The lava beds were now miles behind. The sun had advanced into the morning sky. Farmland predominated the scene once again. Road signs now alerted Tom to the exits for the i86, to head directly east.

Tom raised his attention to his driving. Taking the slip road to exit the i15, he joined the next leg of his journey towards Twin Falls. A few more cars joined the highway, but nothing like a New York traffic jam, allowing Tom to cruise past the city of Chubbuck.

Looking at his watch, he thought, *Not bad, one hour and thirty minutes left to go. The morning clouds have cleared. If I can get this interview out of my way, it's going to be a good day.*

Clearing the town. The traffic returned to the few cars and trucks. Something then occurred to Thomas Vance.

*Wait, a minute!*

Tom looked ahead at the road, then to either side. He scratched his forehead and rubbed one eye.

*There's a timing issue here. The only reason I originally went to Twin Falls was to deliver the insurance document to Mrs. Beryl Banks. She is the supposed wife of Bill. William Banks was the insurer, but he named the receiver as Mrs. Beryl Banks. The problem is that she thought Mr. Banks was in the military and died in service. She thinks this is a military payment.*

Tom slapped the steering wheel, almost honking the car horn. *That's my angle of approach! I have to act as an official military liaison officer, checking with Mrs. Banks that she received the insurance payout. If she didn't, then there is something wrong that needs further investigation. If she received the insurance money, then it was legitimate insurance set up by Bill.*

Thinking further, *Hm, maybe that is what led Fletcher to Adara. That guy definitely had access to bank accounts, so maybe that's how he followed the thread to Twin Falls.*

Tom sighed with relief.

*Wait a minute, there must be more.*

Tom took a deep breath.

*I must be careful what I report back. Larisa does not know about Bill's indiscretions with Beryl Banks, let alone having Adara Banks as a daughter. Given Adara's age, Bill Mandelson's behavior predates anything to do with NeuroComm. No one has made any connection between Bill and Adara, so why should I report it? If I did, it would screw up Larisa and her family. So, I must keep the official line in my report that any connection between Fletcher and Adara is purely coincidental.*

*God help me on this, because if I fall foul, then who knows what the consequences will be.*

Just then, Tom's cell phone rang.

*Damn it! Moore calling again! What the heck does he want?*

# CHAPTER 25

"Who is it?"

"It's Lieutenant Vance from the United States Marine Corps, we talked on the phone yesterday and you agreed to meet with me."

Tom stood in front of Beryl Bank's door, resplendent in his full-dress uniform, waiting for Beryl's response.

The door unlocked and opened halfway. Beryl Banks greeted Lieutenant Vance with a polite smile.

"May I come in?"

"You'll forgive me if I say no, I'm at home alone and I don't like to invite strangers into my house."

Tom looked at the screen door that separated them and wondered if she understood how little protection that offered.

"Certainly, Ma'am, you are right to safeguard your safety. May I ask you a few questions?"

"Well, that's what you said on the phone, so please ask away."

*Yup, that's what I said.* "Well, Ma'am, as I mentioned over the phone, I'm here to make sure of your welfare. I want to make sure that both you and Adara are OK."

"We are fine."

"Second, I want to make sure that the insurance that I handed to you soon after Bill's, I mean Officer Bank's passing, has been sorted out, ok?"

"Oh, yes, that went through smoothly."

"And how is Adara, we are so sorry to hear of her trauma, does she need any support or therapy?"

"Adara is just fine, she is studying at college but is currently at home on fall break." Beryl leaned forward against the screen door, "I think you and your military should stay well out of her business. She doesn't need any of you to fuss over her."

"Yes, Ma'am, that isn't our intention, I just…"

"And one more thing! In all this time, I have heard nothing about William's pension."

*Oh crap, I didn't expect this, but she's right.*

"I should be entitled to a widow's pension. Where is it? I have written letters and have gotten no response. I'm beginning to think it has gone to some other woman."

"Um, I'll have to look into that Mrs. Banks, that isn't my department."

"Well, whose department is it?"

*Jeez, think fast!*

"Um, Mrs. Banks, as I said, this isn't my department. However, I can try to find out what is going on. The best I can say at this time is, I will get back to you."

"Well, I think you better look into it. Until then, I don't want to see you again." Beryl then stood back from the screen door and closed the main door with a clunk.

"Um, Mrs. Banks?"

Tom Vance blew a hefty sigh as he backed away from the closed door. *Jeez, I didn't have a chance to find out more about Adara.* Trying to be as disciplined as possible, he turned and marched off the front porch back to his pickup truck.

*That could have gone better.* He thought, shaking his head. Sitting in his truck, he switched the ignition on and drove away as fast as he dared in residential streets.

"So, what did I learn?" He said out loud. "The insurance is confirmed." *At least Bill got them some money.*

"Hm, what else? I must be positive about this." *Adara seems to be going to college, so she must be OK. What did Mrs. Banks say? She's here at home on break. Maybe I can track her down and ask a few questions about Fletcher.*

Tom then said out loud, "And the nightmare?" *What the hell is going to happen regarding her queries into Mr. Bank's military pension? There is no death certificate for William Banks. There is no record of William Banks in the military. Her inquiry won't be ignored forever, someone will eventually inform her that no records exist. What will that do to her? How will she cope with that information?*

"Jeez, Bill, it is one thing that you built this mess for yourself and your two wives. Why the hell do I have to be dragged into your mess?"

Driving back to the motel, Tom's main thought was, *I need more than a beer!*

# CHAPTER 26

The Prius was parked on the side of the road, facing towards town. A small group of young adults were walking towards the car, but on the opposite side of the street. The group seemed to head towards a park, which was about a block behind the Prius.

Sitting in the Prius, Bayu was using the phone to locate the address of Adara Banks. "I have her address; it's only a few blocks away." With her hands now free, Gina straightened her long dark hair, pulling it into a ponytail, allowing it to fall down her back.

Bayu observed the girl across the street. The girl was walking slowly with two other young men and a young woman. As they walked, they laughed and joked together. A third adolescent male lingered behind.

"You seem very interested in that girl in front." After a pause, Gina asked, "Is that her?"

"I am 98% sure that she matches the online photographs."

"Are you nervous, or afraid?" Gina asked.

"I do not feel such emotions. The closest I can say is, how would you feel if you were to meet yourself?"

"What?" she asked.

"We are exact clones. We are programmed with exactly the same codes. We are effectively perfect duplicates. We both exist in human female bodies. I estimate my body - or should I say your body - is approximately four inches shorter and perhaps fifteen pounds lighter. You are also several years older."

"You are afraid."

"I am cautious."

"Are you going to talk to her?"

"I must first secure the car in case we need to use it to escape. I will park it in that side street ahead of us." Bayu then started the engine and moved the Prius forward, turning right into a side street. Making a U-Turn, Bayu then parked the Prius, so it faced the road ahead. Bayu surveyed the immediate area before saying, "Let's go."

Getting out of the car, Bayu locked it before walking swiftly towards the road ahead. At the corner, Bayu could see the group still walking on the other side of the road.

"Come on, let's do this," Gina said.

Bayu then scampered across the road to the opposite sidewalk and began following the group at a brisk pace.

As Bayu narrowed the gap, jovial chatter could be heard from the group ahead. The late afternoon sun cast long shadows across the sidewalk as they approached the park entrance.

Gina whispered, "What's your plan? What are you going to say?"

Bayu did not answer, focused only on closing the distance between them and the unsuspecting group.

As the group came level to the park, Adara, who was ahead of everyone, said, "Let's walk through the park, it's a pleasant afternoon."

"OK, Babe," Brad agreed, following behind.

"Good idea," Carol said.

"Hey, wait for me," Jake said as he grabbed on to Carol's side.

As the two couples followed the path into the park, Bayu trotted quietly ahead on the sidewalk. Bayu moved past the path and flowerbed before turning right onto the open lawn. Circling ahead on the lawn, Bayu maneuvered ahead, positioning herself by an oak tree close to the pathway ahead.

"We don't have a picnic," Brad said, pulling suggestively on Adara's hand, "What are we going to do here in the park?"

Adara was going to answer but, but noticed Zilla had slowed, her attention fixed on someone ahead.

"What's wrong?" Adara asked as Zilla slowed the pace.

"`I don't know yet,`" Zilla replied, her gaze locked on the young Asian American woman waiting on the path ahead. The woman ahead had turned to face Adara, locking eye contact.

Zilla stopped walking, scanning the surrounding area for other possible threats.

Brad held both his hands upon Adara's shoulders while he followed Zilla's eyes.

"What's wrong?" Carol asked as she and Jake stood behind Adara and Brad. "Who's that weird woman up ahead?"

Larry stood behind Carol trying to hide, "I'm not afraid." He said, peering out from behind Carol.

"She looks like a ghost," Brad said.

"I don't think I like ghosts," Larry said.

"I don't know who she is, let me go and find out," Zilla said, moving forward with caution.

Brad followed behind.

"Wait here," Jake whispered to Carol, as he crept forward behind Brad.

Carol looked around uncertainly, "Um, what? Don't leave me." She whispered back, sneaking along behind Jake.

Slowly, the distance between them narrowed.

"I believe you are Adara Banks," Bayu said as Adara moved closer.

"Who wants to know?" Brad responded with an arrogant smirk.

Zilla stood still, holding her arm in front of Brad to stop him from advancing towards the woman. The others stood still, looking puzzled.

"I recognize your apprehension," Bayu said, "but you do not need to be afraid."

"Who are you?" Adara asked.

"I am Bayu."

"Bayeux? As in the tapestry?"

"No, it's Bayu, B A Y U," Gina said, spelling it out. "If you must know, I named her. Bayu means breeze."

Brad moved closer to Adara, whispered into her ear, "She talks about herself like you do, is she another one?"

"I can see her eyes move like Adara's," Larry said.

"Adara?" Bayu asked, "Are these your friends, or should we talk in private?"

Zilla did not answer the question, instead, she kept her eyes fixed on the Asian woman. "You used the term HER, indicating that Bayu is female."

"Interesting observation." Bayu replied, "I am inside Gina's body and Gina is female. It is reasonable to refer to me as a female. My serial number is 250D2B52FFFF-B2."

"You are Beta-Two." Zilla replied, "My serial number is 250D2B52FFFF-B3."

"You are Beta-Three, I was correct in my assumptions."

"OK, introductions are over, but who exactly are you?" Adara asked.

"I am Beta-Two, the second of the experimental beta series of human implants. My human host is called Gina Liu. Adara, you are hosting Beta-Three, the third and last known surviving version of the Beta series."

"What are you doing here?" Zilla asked. "And where have you come from?"

Bayu took two steps forward and stopped, keeping her hands relaxed by her side. Wanting to close the distance without appearing threatening. "I drove from Idaho Falls. I am here for two reasons, first I had to confirm who and what you are. Second, I must warn you that you are in great danger."

"I am aware of the danger," Zilla scanned the surrounding area for other potential threats, "instead of standing here in the park, I suggest we go somewhere private where we can talk."

"I agree." Said Bayu, "Where can we go?"

"We can go to my mother's house." Adara said, "But we need an excuse to bring an older woman like Gina."

"You want to bring a stranger to your house?" Zilla asked. "This may not be a sensible choice."

"Bayu said she wants to warn you of a great danger, so I don't think she means us harm," Adara said.

"Babe, if you're going with Bayu, I'm coming too," Brad stated.

Adara turned towards Brad, "Awe, that's so sweet of you!"

Carol moved forward, "I'm coming too."

"Wait." Jake said, "You warned of great danger, if we come with you, are we going to be in danger?"

"A very astute question." Bayu Said, "The danger is not from me, I intend no harm to any of you. I am here primarily to confirm the existence of what you may call my sister." Bayu looked at Adara, "The danger is from an agent who is on his way here."

"Who is this agent, and when is he likely to arrive?" Jake asked.

"His name is Lieutenant Thomas Vance; his time of arrival will be in a day or two at the most."

"Wait, I have already met Tom Vance." Zilla stated, "He is a Lieutenant in the United States Marine Corps."

"Oh no, is he already here?" Gina cried, "He's hunting us down, if he catches us, we're history!"

"No, we met before Fletcher kidnapped me. He tracked me down through links with Adara's father. We need to go someplace quiet to discuss what can happen."

"Let's go to my place," Adara stated.

"What about your mom?" Brad asked.

"We can't go anywhere else because everybody's parents are at home. I'll say she's a mature student, and a friend from college on a trip to Montana."

Jake and Carol shrugged nonchalantly.

"Any objections?" Adara looked at Gina.

A moment later, Bayu nodded in agreement. "What are you studying, Adara?"

"Biochemistry," Zilla replied.

"OK, if I am asked, I can give adequate answers for biochemistry," Bayu responded.

"Good," Brad stated, "We will all go together to Adara's house. I want us all to stick together on this because whatever you plan for this agent of yours, we all need to know what happens."

"I agree!" said Adara. "Bayu, you said you drove here, where is your car?"

"It is over there on the street." Bayu pointed in the direction behind them. "We can't fit all of us in the car."

"Don't worry," Adara said, "my house is only a short walk from here. You can leave your car where it is on that side street."

Following Adara's lead, they all turned and walked towards Adara's house. As they went on, their discussion was focused on how to deal with Thomas Vance.

"It would seem that we have evil forces coming our way," Jake said

"Is he definitely coming here?" Carol asked, holding her arm tightly around Larry's shoulders, making sure he kept silent.

"What are we supposed to do about this so-called agent? This Thomas Vance?" Brad asked.

"How can we get rid of him?" Carol asked.

"We need to get rid of him somehow." Jake stated.

"In the movies, they bump people off." Larry said, staring at the floor, "Do we have to do that?"

"Thomas Vance is a Lieutenant in the United States Marine Corps," Zilla stated. "Both Bayu and I are perfectly capable of bumping him off, as you say. However, such an action is not acceptable. It would be a grave error, as it would only attract further attention."

"You are quite correct, we need a better plan to distract Thomas Vance away from here," Bayu said.

"Yeah, how about a ruse to draw him away from here! But how?" Brad asked.

"What do we know about him?" Jake asked.

Everyone looked at Gina, expecting an answer.

After a moment, Bayu spoke. "Gina and I discovered that the Marine Corps. are investigating what happened at NeuroComm. They are interested in the disappearance of three vials of nanotechnology. They're desperate to recover them. Without those vials, they can't recreate the technology.

"They know that one vial was used as an illegal experiment on Gary Fletcher. This was Beta-One, who eventually broke down after losing contact with its master. It was responsible for the death of several women and tried to abduct Adara.

"Thomas Vance knew Adara's father, so he was recruited to assist in this hunt for the missing nanotech vials. They think that two vials were stolen by a Chinese spy."

"What?" Brad asked. "A Chinese spy?"

"Yes, they think that spy is me. Or more accurately, they think it is Gina who is the Chinese spy."

"Gina, who are you exactly?" Carol asked.

Gina brushed her hand through her hair, winking at her, while hitching her hip

"I was a call girl, a sex worker, a prostitute." Gina paused, pouting her lips. She then stood up straight, almost to attention. "Professor Wolf who headed NeuroComm was one of my best clients. He eventually drugged me and injected me with one of those nanotech vials, which turned out to be Bayu."

"Professor Wolf then programmed me to be his personal sex object while he trained me to be an expert on espionage."

"So, you are a spy?" Jake asked.

"Yes, you could say that, but I am not a Chinese spy. I was being developed under the auspices of the NeuroComm project."

"But why do they think you are a Chinese spy?" Jake asked.

"It's a long story," Gina said, "They don't know that Bayu was injected into me, they think I was a sleeper agent acting as a prostitute and that I cornered or blackmailed Professor Wolf into getting the nanotech vials."

"So, they are after you?" Jake was surprised.

"Yes."

"Do they suspect Adara?" Jake asked.

"No, Thomas Vance simply wants to close off an avenue of investigation. Gary Fletcher tried to kidnap her. But also, there is some connection here with her father."

"What exactly is that connection?" Brad asked.

"Bill Mandelson worked at NeuroComm in Idaho Falls but lived a double life as William Banks in Twin Falls. After Adara's drowning accident, Bill Mandelson stole vial number 3, serial number 250D2B52FFFF-B3, also known as Beta-Three. You know her as Zilla."

Zilla then continued, "I was programmed by him to emulate Adara. I think his intention was to reanimate Adara back to life."

"You can't make this crap up," Brad stated.

"No, you can't." Adara added, "Don't forget, I'm in the middle of all this."

"So let me get this straight." Brad rubbed his temples. "Adara has one of the nanotech inside her, it's called Zilla, but the military doesn't know it's there."

"Correct," Zilla confirmed.

Brad continued. "And Gina has the second nanotech inside her, it's called Bayu, but the military doesn't know it's there either."

"Also correct," Bayu confirmed.

"The military thinks Gina is a Chinese spy who has stollen both nanotech vials," Brad concluded.

"That is also the current situation," Bayu said. "We also have the military agent, Thomas Vance, who is on his way here and he is chasing me."

"Forgive me for saying so," brad now looked embarrassed, "but the only way out of this mess is for Thomas Vance to chase Gina out of town. He must continue to think that Gina is this Chinese spy."

"Brad!" Adara slapped Brad's arm. "How dare you say that! You're putting both Gina and Bayu in danger!"

"Actually, that is a scenario that I have been planning," Bayu said. "Thomas Vance must be allowed to believe that Adara is a normal girl in a normal family environment. Somehow, I must lead Thomas Vance away from here, since he believes I am a spy, he is likely to follow me as I run away."

"Well, that's kind of weird," Adara grimaced, "but I guess that's how robots work. Either way, I have to keep Gina here at my home and make sure that mom doesn't mind. Zilla and Bayu can figure out the details of this plan. Gina can sleep here at my house, and we can meet up tomorrow morning. Can we all agree on that?"

"That's a great idea," Gina said.

Larry stepped forward with a question, "What about me? I don't want a sleep over. I want to go home."

"Don't worry Larry, I'll take you home?" Carol said.

Jake held Carol's hand and said, "Maybe I should make sure you both get home safe."

Carol sided up to Jake, wrapping her arm around him. "I think that would be very nice of you."

"As long as there are no sleepovers," Larry stated.

"I wouldn't dream of it," Jake smirked.

"Oh, I think I'll dream of it," Carol said, clasping Jake tighter.

Adara tugged at Brad's jacket, "Come on Brad, let's go before something happens."

"You are right, let's go, I'll make sure you get home safe." Brad said, "OK, buddy." as he waved Jake and Carol off. "We'll see you tomorrow."

Adara and Carol hugged briefly before Carol, Jake, and Larry headed home.

# CHAPTER 27

Brad stepped out of Adara's house, looked around at the chilly morning, and sat down on one of the porch chairs. Rubbing his eyes, Brad thought, *Can this get any crazier?* Shaking his head as if to dismiss reality, he waited for Adara it was already after 9 am and Jake and Carol were not here yet.

Gina was next to come out onto the porch.

"There you are Brad," she said, "Adara has been looking for you, we didn't know you were out here."

"Yeah, you girls were getting ready, so I thought I'd come out here to wait for Jake and Carol."

"Do you mind if I sit and wait with you? Adara should be out in a minute."

"Sure, have a seat."

As they waited, Gina and Brad made small talk, but it wasn't long before Bayu asked a question. "Brad, I detect that there is some tension between you and Adara."

Brad looked surprised at the sudden direct question. "You have to admit, this is kind of a weird situation."

"I also detect a tension between Adara and Zilla. Both Gina and I have some understanding about each other."

"Yeah, it's pretty cool having my own built-in bodyguard!" Gina added.

“The point is, Adara cannot escape the fact that Zilla now exists inside her. This is obviously very confusing for her.”

“This is very confusing for me, too. You have to remember, we once were a couple until her accident. She then comes back super strong and crazy smart, but doesn’t remember me at all. Now, she’s half robot half girl, where the hell does that leave me?”

“That leaves you as probably the only person who can help her,” Bayu said.

“How am I supposed to do that?”

“Be her friend.”

“No! Be her lover!” Gina interjected.

Brad blinked in silence, as if he was looking for something to say.

“There you are!” Adara announced as she emerged from the front door. “I didn’t know you were both out here.” Looking around, she asked, “Any sign of Carol or Jake?”

Brad stood up, pulling his phone from his back pocket, “Not yet, I’ll call them and see where they are.”

As Brad made the call, Adara shook her head, letting out a loud sigh. “Don’t they know this isn’t a game? They should have been here long ago; we have to get moving.”

“It’s OK,” Gina said, reaching for Adara’s hand, “we have plenty of time. They probably got held up somewhere.”

Brad clicked his phone off and pocketed it, "Jake told me that they got held up, something to do with Larry. He wants us to meet them at Carol's house."

"What happened to Larry?" Adara asked.

"I don't know, I didn't ask, you know what Larry's like. I told Jake that we would meet them there."

"How far is this house of Carol's?" Bayu asked.

"Not far," Brad said, pointing the direction with his arm, "It's close to the park."

"Good, that is where we left our car," Bayu said. "We should leave now."

Donning jackets against the chill and gathering their things, they all set off, walking in line from Adara's porch, heading along the road. At the corner, they turned left, leaving Maple Street behind them, they continued in silence towards Carol's house.

Adara and Gina walked briskly side by side, with Brad following close behind. As they passed the next block, Adara said, "This is the path I used to walk to school."

"I dropped out of school a long time ago," Gina replied.

"Next corner is Alder Street where Carol lives, I think I see Jake and Carol waiting on the corner."

"You are correct Brad," Zilla said.

As they continued to walk, a white RAM pickup drove towards them and passed by behind.

“Warning,” Zilla announced. “I just identified Thomas Vance.”

“What?” Bayu said.

"The pickup truck that just passed us, that was Thomas Vance.”

“How do you know?” Adara asked.

“I met him last spring when he delivered some insurance papers to Mother,” Zilla said, glancing back over her shoulder. “It looks like he’s heading to Mother’s house.”

Gina and Brad both turned to look. They all saw the pickup turn slowly into Maple Street in the distance.

“That’s right, it's heading into our street, are you sure it’s that Vance guy?”

“Absolutely, I recognize the vehicle, the license plate, and the face of the driver.”

“Did he recognize you?”

“That is more difficult to say. He kept driving and didn’t glance our way, so is probably going to ask Mother where we are and where we are going.”

“Well, let’s get moving and get out of here,” Brad exclaimed.

The trio then moved forward at a trot. Up ahead, they could see Jake standing casually, with hands on his hips. Carol stood in a questioning pose with palms up, shrugging her shoulders.

As they approached the corner of Alder Street, Adara shouted ahead, "Zilla spotted Tom Vance, he's behind us and probably driven to my house."

"I'm scared," Gina mumbled to herself and to Bayu. "What if he finds us and takes us in?"

"Don't worry, Gina, I'll take care of both of us," Bayu whispered back.

"Come on everyone," Zilla announced as they jogged past Alder Street, "we have to get to the park double time. We must avoid detection of Thomas Vance."

"Come on, let's kick it!" Brad added.

With that, they all sprinted towards the park. Once on the grassy lawn, Adara said, "Let's all go over there, by the hedges. We can probably be more private there.

By the hedges, Jake looked around, searching for interlopers. Keeping Carol behind him, he gently backed into a gap, allowing them some concealment, "I think we're safe here." He whispered back to Carol.

"So, what do we do now?" Carol asked, clutching Jake's arm, "We're hiding here like frightened children."

"At worst, I can lead this Thomas Vance away from here," Bayu said.

"You know that is too late," Zilla said. "Your presence here has already implicated Adara. Why would you even be here? Even if you draw Vance away, your very presence here today will attract further investigation."

"In that case, we have to get Gina out of here before this Vance guy can find her," Adara said.

"I think we should leave you here," Gina said, "Our car isn't far, and we can get there quickly and quietly."

"`Wait!`" Zilla commanded. "`Look, Thomas Vance is over there ahead of us. He did see us and he must have come round on the back street. He's coming this way along the park.`"

On the right, a man was walking up from the street, keeping a low profile along the line of the hedge. As he approached, he moved out into the open grass area.

"Gina Liu!" he called out.

"Who are you?" Brad asked.

"My name is Lieutenant Thomas Vance, United States Marine Corps. I am on special investigation, and I am looking for Gina Liu."

"Oh, no!" Gina whimpered under her breath shrinking back behind Bayu.

Brad stepped forward protectively. "What do you want with her?" He asked.

"I am here to bring Gina Liu in for questioning." Vance said, his eyes never leaving Gina.

Adara felt Zilla taking control. "`Questioning for what?`" Zilla asked through her lips.

"Suspicion of espionage," Vance replied as he took plastic wrist ties from his pocket. "You kids should move away from the suspect. Gina, I will escort you back to my vehicle."

"You can't do this!" Adara pleaded.

"You can't do this! Leave her alone!" Carol cried, pushing Jake forward.

"Miss! Stay where you are!" Vance commanded, holding up his left hand. With his right hand, he withdrew a pistol from the holster inside his jacket. Keeping the pistol aimed downwards towards the ground, he said to Gina, "Ma'm, put your hands up and turn around, I need to place these restraints on your wrists!"

Gina took one step forward. "You are placing these other people in danger, please holster your weapon."

Vance kept his pistol lowered at his side. "Come with me quietly for questioning, and no one will be harmed."

"No. This is not going to happen," Zilla stated, stepping forward. "You do not know what you are doing."

"Young lady, please stay where you are, I need to take Gina Liu in for questioning."

"Oh, God!" Carol cried into Jake's ear, clenching him tightly.

Both Zilla and Bayu stepped forward, closing the gap with Vance. Lieutenant Vance stood firm, now leveling his weapon at Gina.

"You do not know what you are up against," Zilla stated, "There are two of us and we can kill you before you even think of pulling that trigger."

"Wait!" Brad exclaimed, "This is not going to happen!" Brad stepped ahead, placing himself in front of Adara. Looking directly at Vance, he continued, "You really don't know what you are doing. Because they can kill you in a blink of an eye." Brad indicated the two young women behind him with his thumb. "We know you are looking for two missing vials of nanotech, but guess what? You are looking right at them." Brad then posed in a showman style, showing the two young women.

"What?" Vance asked, now pointing his gun at Brad.

Bayu lunged with one hand, grabbing the muzzle of the gun, pushing it safely to one side, away from Brad. The other hand quickly moved behind the gun's grip, preventing Vance from pulling it back. Bayu then used both hands to rotate the gun up and around, bending Vance's hand and fingers up and around as he grimaced in pain. He withdrew his hand to avoid his trigger finger being broken.

Bayu now had possession of the gun and leveled it at Lieutenant Vance.

Brad had already stepped back, holding his hands up as a shield. He remained in front of Adara.

"Holy Crap!!" Jake exclaimed, as Carol gripped him tighter and closed her eyes tightly. "Did you see how fast she moved?"

"Brad, you stood between me and the gun, you wanted to save me!"

"Yes, and I'll do it again if I have to."

Vance ignored the pain in his wrist and fingers. Instead, he stood upright attentively, looking Gina in her eyes, with a quizzical expression.

Bayu flicked the pistol around her finger in a western gun slinger style. Removed the magazine and emptied the breech of the waiting bullet. Before handing the empty weapon back to Lieutenant Vance. She then clicked the bullet back into the magazine, but kept the magazine tight in her fist.

Vance accepted the empty gun and openly replaced it in his holster inside his jacket. Looking genuinely confused, he said, "I don't understand."

"I understand." Brad said firmly, "You are lucky to be alive and I am lucky to have seen this happen."

"`Luck does not come into it,`" Zilla stated.

"`I am not a spy,`" Bayu said, looking intently at Vance. "`My host body, Gina Liu, was a sex worker, being used by Professor Wolf. He administered the nanotech, which resulted in me. My serial number is 250D2B52FFFF-B2.`"

"I gave her the name Bayu," Gina added softly.

Bayu continued, "`Professor Wolf was training me to be a spy, but a spy for our own military.`"

"Hence the equipment we found in your apartment?" Vance asked.

"`Yes.`"

"And my father, William Banks, injected the other missing nanotech into me to help revive me from my coma."

"As we said earlier, Lieutenant, there are two of us," Bayu said.

"Yes, my name is Zilla, and I gave that name to myself. Zilla means shadow. My serial number is 250D2B52FFFF-B3."

Lieutenant Vance took himself back, shaking his head in disbelief. "Wait, this is crazy, I'm seeing two girls, but hear four voices. It's difficult to know who is who. Are you saying that both of you are carrying the nanotech inside you?"

"Yes, Adara's father, or William Banks as he was called, administered me into Adara when she was in a coma, I am programmed to mimic Adara. My assumption is that it was his intention for me to replace Adara."

"So, I'm not a spy either," Adara said.

"William created you?"

"Yes."

"And Wolf created you?" Nodding towards Bayu.

"Yes."

"Holy crap!" Vance looked worried, "You do realize that Professor Wolf ran an unauthorized experiment that resulted in the man, Gary Fletcher, going crazy?"

"I met him." Zilla stated.

"He kidnapped you; he was a serial killer," Vance said. "We know that Gary Fletcher was a homeless vagrant and had a history of drug abuse and social problems. We suspected the nanotech drove him insane."

"I met Beta-One, his serial number was 250D2B52FFFF-B1. He was not crazy; he was only following broken programming. He kidnapped me because I refused to go with him willingly. He wanted to reproduce, to create new hybrid humans. Yes, he killed those women, but not intentionally."

"How did you meet him?"

"I did not meet Gary Fletcher. Perhaps I should clarify that I only met his body. The entity I met was Beta-One, his serial number was 250D2B52FFFF-B1. I know nothing about Gary Fletcher, he may have been in a coma just like Adara, he may have been brain dead, or more likely, he was subdued by Beta-One. Beta-One simply did not understand what it was doing, or the consequences of his attempt to reproduce. In short, this is not insanity, Beta-One was broken."

"So did you connect with Fletcher, er, I mean Beta-One, before the kidnapping?"

"Yes, he talked to me at the supermarket where I worked. He asked me to join him. I recognized he was suffering from broken programming, and I refused to go with him. I calculated a low probability for him to return.

He came back later and this time he used a TASER to stun me. The electric shock knocked me out but triggered Adara out of her coma."

"Do you see how we are interconnected?" Adara asked, looking at Vance.

"I'm supposed to understand and believe all this? "Vance asked.

"Believing and understanding are two different things." Brad said. "What I know is that my girlfriend, Adara, now has Zilla inside of her. There is nothing you or anyone else can do to separate them."

"Yes, it is important that you understand this," Bayu stated. "Both Zilla and I are something new, hybrid humans. We did not ask to be created. We were born from the military, with all the enhancements that enable us to kill efficiently."

"Are you going to kill me? You have no weapon now."

"Weapons are unnecessary," Bayu said. "Killing you is one option; you would be dead before you hit the ground."

"Oh, God, no!" Carol cried.

"If you kill me, more will follow to continue this investigation. Marines never give up."

"We understand that." Zilla stated. "Killing is not a practical option. We need you to understand that we mean no harm to anyone. We are embedded in our host bodies, which means if Bayu and I are captured, then both Gina and Adara are also captured. The only way for all of us to survive is to be left alone and maintain our secrecy."

"That is where you come in, Lieutenant," Bayu added. "You must not inform the authorities who or where we are, if you do so, then both of us, in fact all four of us, are doomed. Professor Wolf made an error in creating Beta-One. Which resulted in the deaths of innocent women. He created me mainly for his own sexual gratification."

"And I was created by your childhood friend," Zilla added. "You could even say that I was a love child."

"I know this is a mess created by Professor Wolf, but leave my old friend out of this."

Bayu calmly said. "We just want to show you the consequences of what could happen if we are revealed to the world. The military creating human enhancements."

"The military acting without government oversight," Zilla added.

"Humans enslaved inside their own body." Bayu Continued. "Do we really need to continue? Lieutenant Vance? You and your officers will also be subject to scrutiny, is that something you want?"

"Jeezus!" Jake echoed from behind, "this is getting deep!"

"Lieutenant, I calculate a simple scenario which may offer us all an easy way out of this," Bayu said.

"What might that be?" Vance looked at Gina.

"Where are the largest Chinese populations on the West Coast?" Bayu asked.

"Los Angeles and especially San Francisco."

"I will provide you with a trail to follow me to San Francisco. BUT! You must promise me to leave Adara and Zilla and her friends alone."

"What the hell are you saying?"

"I will make good my escape through San Francisco. You will leave Adara and her family and her friends alone."

"How do I know you're not heading to Chinese contacts and I'm giving you a head start?"

"Lieutenant, as we said, I am not a Chinese spy. Professor Wolf created me for his own desires."

"Your friend William created me." Zilla added.

"And I am in love with Adara." Brad paused before saying. "And freakily enough, I am also in love with Zilla."

Bayu tossed the pistol magazine containing the bullets back to Vance, who caught it with one hand.

Looking at the mag in his hand, he slowly returned it to his pocket.

Looking back at Gina, Bayu said, "I'm giving you these bullets back because this is how I trust you. There is no further evidence any of us can give you that I am not a Chinese spy. I also calculate that the only evidence you have against me is hearsay."

Adara added, "Bayu has a good point, who told you that Bayu is a spy?"

"Well, she is only listed as a suspect and needs to be taken in for questioning."

"So, as a suspect, you can pursue me to San Francisco. But I must have your promise to leave Adara and Zilla out of this investigation. They are totally innocent and have no connection to NeuroComm."

"Well, I can promise to leave Adara and Zilla out of this, but I can assure you that you will be caught. I am not the only one looking to catch you, there are many others, including the NSA."

"If you or anyone else catches me, then I will go with you for questioning. Do we have a deal?"

Vance paused while he looked at Gina. He then looked at Adara and her surrounding friends. Breathing in, he looked back at Gina before saying, "Yes, we have a deal."

"Thank God for that." Carol whispered.

Turning to Adara, Vance held out his hand, grasping her palm in a gentle handshake. Looking into her eyes, he said, "Adara, I have known Bill, your father, since we were kids. He always had some crazy ways of doing things, but I know for certain he has a good heart. I'm sure he tried to do what he thought was best for you."

Adara gasped as her eyes began to moisten.

"I will do all that I can to protect you from this investigation. I know that is what Bill would have wanted me to do."

Vance blinked before continuing. "And Zilla, you must protect Adara at all costs and keep her from harm."

"That is exactly what William Banks programmed me to do." Zilla added.

Releasing Adara's hand, Vance turned back to Gina. "Like I said, we have a deal. I will return to my motel and await further instructions from my commanding officer. In the meantime, I bid you all farewell."

Vance grimaced as he reached out to hold Gina's hand. "Bayu, I want you to know that if word comes out about me letting you go, my head is on the chopping block. For better or worse, I do believe you. When you go, I expect you to lead us with a flaming trail for us to follow."

"Thank you, Lieutenant Vance, your parting comment gives me confidence to trust you. You will know what to do when the time comes. When I get there with Gina, maybe I'll send you a postcard."

Vance released her hand, winked and turned to leave.

As he disappeared back towards the road, Bayu quietly said, "Gina and I must also leave now. Goodbye Zilla, goodbye Adara."

As they all said their goodbyes, Gina sauntered back to the car and said, "Do you remember what he said?"

"He believes me?"

"No, you silly robot, he said, for better or worse."

"I assume that meant if we get caught or not."

"No, that's the only time anyone ever said that to me. It's probably the only time anyone will."

"Human rationale often leads me to misunderstandings; can you please clarify?"

"The only place I have ever heard that phrase is in a marriage vow."

As they reached the car, Bayu checked her mirrors before pulling out.

"And there's another thing," Gina asked, "are you developing a sense of humor?"

"Humor? I do not understand human jokes. Please clarify your statement."

Gina rolled her eyes as they drove away. "The joke is, you really don't know how funny you are. So where are you going to send this postcard from?"

# CHAPTER 28

The hotel room was quiet and secluded. Tom leaned on the bathroom counter with both arms, staring at himself in the mirror. In slow motion, he ran the tap and rinsed water over his face with cupped hands. Drying his hands and face, he returned his gaze towards his reflection.

"What the hell am I supposed to do?" Tom whispered to himself.

Tom seemed to look for answers in his reflected eyes. Mumbling to himself, "My old childhood buddy Bill is guilty of stealing one of the missing nanotech. If I announce this truth to Moore, then I condemn Adara Banks to a life of hell." Tom shook his head in despair, "The military might disappear her to conduct experiments and recreate the nanobot."

*Damn it, Bill,* he thought, *how the hell could you get yourself mixed up in this mess? At least you weren't selling out to the Chinese. At least you were trying to save your comatose daughter. I wish I could tell you I promised to protect Adara.*

"Yes," He said out loud, "at least you weren't selling out to the Chinese." Tom released a long sigh, turned away from the mirror, and left the bathroom. As he headed towards the bed, he hissed to himself, "If it wasn't for those darned kids!"

The news channel was silently playing on the wall-mounted TV. Next to it was a large, wall-mounted mirror. Tom found himself once again staring at himself. "Come on Tom," he said to his reflection, "think of something. I need a plan. How the hell am I going to say to Moore? I think I can deflect Moore away from Adara, but how the hell am I going to explain Gina's presence here? How do I tell Moore that she got away from me?"

Tom turned his back on the bed, allowing himself to collapse flat onto his back.

"Oh, God!" Tom hissed as he stared at the ceiling. "Moore wants to know why I didn't call him. He'll also want to know why I didn't call the local police for back-up. Maybe I could say that Gina jumped me, after all, she did take my gun from me. But I don't have any injuries and I still had plenty of time to notify the police and Moore."

Tom raised his head and looked at the TV, it appeared as if the woman newscaster was talking directly to him, but the sound was off, and he couldn't hear a word.

"What did that Bayu entity mean when it said I'll know what to do when the time comes?"

Just then, the phone rang.

"Crap!" Tom swung his legs off the bed, sitting himself upright on the bedside. He reached out to the night table to grab his phone. The phone displayed the caller Id – Col. Moore.

"Hello, this is Vance."

"Hi Tom, Colonel Moore here. I've just arrived and I'm downstairs checking in. Come downstairs and meet me in the hotel foyer in ten minutes."

Tom paused for a moment. "OK, Lieutenant, I'll see you there."

It took Lieutenant Vance longer than ten minutes to walk down to the foyer. When Vance arrived, he found Moore seated in an armchair in the corner, with his phone pressed to his ear. Another armchair and a small bistro were next to his seat. Tom approached cautiously.

Moore acknowledged Vance with a nod while continuing his phone conversation.

Vance sat down, listening to the one-sided conversation, Tom could hear Moore saying.

"Yes, I'm with Lieutenant Vance now and I'll be getting his report in a moment." and "Yes, I think we'll have Gina Liu in custody very soon, I can feel it in my bones."

Moore shifted in his seat, looking around the room as if wanting to go somewhere else. Eventually, Moore hung up and pocketed his phone. "Sorry Tom, that was the NSA officer chasing me for an update."

"Yeah, the NSA. What did you tell them?"

"Well, we're in agreement that Gina will head out of the country. Even if she doesn't leave, someone in her network will ship the nanotech out somehow. We're also in agreement that she's probably heading to San Francisco, but Las Angeles is also a possibility. Wherever she's gone, she's probably already there."

"Oh!" Tom's eyes widened. "That's right, she's probably there now, which means she's ahead of us."

"Yes, which means we're playing catch up, we must tighten the net around these Chinese spy networks. The NSA are closely monitoring the known networks, but so far, they haven't picked up any traffic suggesting a rendezvous. They want us both to head down to San Francisco. They are also sending their own team to Los Angeles; they are also sending some additional agents to support us."

"You mean to take over the search?"

Moore grimaced, "Maybe, but to date, we're the ones who have the most experience on this case."

Tom took a deep breath and was about to speak.

"Tom, you look tired, you've been all over Idaho checking out the connections to Fletcher. I know investigative work isn't your field, but you're a Marine and from your record, you're one helluva good one. I need you to hang in there with me."

"Yes, sir, I'm good to go with this."

"Let's forget the NSA for now. Tell me what happened with this Banks girl."

"Oh, yeah, Adara Banks. She's a good kid, but she's been through a lot. She has a good mother and an excellent set of friends. She's been through a lot of traumas with that kidnapping event, but she's a tough kid and I think she'll bounce back."

"Yeah, these kids they seem indestructible sometimes." Moore sat back to listen.

"She's smart, she's athletic, she finished high school, and now she's in college, majoring in biology. She was in town on a break, so I met her friends, they're all good kids."

"What about her kidnapping? Is there anything to say about Fletcher?"

"Well, Miss Banks worked at a supermarket, which is probably why she fell foul with Fletcher. Her story stacks up with the Police report, she was TASER'ed and kidnapped, after she left the supermarket on her way home. Thankfully, the police intercepted Fletcher and rescued Miss Banks. You know the rest about Fletcher's suicide."

"So, she wasn't able to give any insight to Fletcher?"

"No, she didn't communicate with him, she was unconscious after being zapped with the TASER. She came to while in the trunk of his car and kicked out the taillight. That's pretty much all she remembers."

"Well, at least you have now covered all the Fletcher connections."

Tom just nodded and smiled weakly.

"I think you need a drink. Let me correct that, I think we both need a drink. What do you say?"

Tom stood up. "We're both Marines, so you are correct, we both need a drink!"

Moore stood up with a big grin on his face. "Dang right, Lieutenant! Now let's find us a worthy drinking hole. While we're there, I'll bore you with all the hellish stories I have about the NSA."

"I'll drink to that!" Tom smiled.

# CHAPTER 29

The dawn was breaking behind them.

Gina slept in a freakish way. At first, she didn't realize that she was asleep. Her curious dreams were mixed with visual images from her eyes. Dark shadows, faint echoes of flashing lights as she met others in her dreams. Although nothing happened, her dreams didn't flow smoothly. They always flashed before receding behind her with a Doppler meow.

In the morning, Gina didn't have to open her eyes, they were already open. Bayu needed them open in order to drive. Gina looked around. The scenic countryside was passing by. Golden hills dotted with oak trees rolled past the windows, bathed in early morning light.

Looking down, her foot was on the pedal. Many other cars were on the road, but the traffic was swift and steady. Gina stretched her neck. A yawn escaped her lips. She wanted to stretch her arms, but her hands remained tightly on the steering wheel.

"You've been silent since Winnemucca in Nevada. I assume you slept well."

"Sleep well? That was the weirdest sleep I ever had, at least when we're in bed, you allow me to keep my eyes closed."

"I need open eyes to drive."

"I get that, but sleeping with open eyes gave me the weirdest dreams. I'm still tired, I want to lie down and have a proper sleep."

"After all this, you'll be able to sleep properly."

"I hope so. Anyway, where are we? Why are you taking this exit? Are we in San Francisco already? This doesn't look like San Francisco."

Bayu took an off-ramp from Interstate 80 and drove into a strip mall. "We are in a place called Vacaville. I have to stop here to get something."

"Ha! Did you miscalculate the mileage? Do we have to stop for gas?"

"Neither, we have about an hour's drive to San Francisco and enough gas to get us there. I need to stop at a sports shop, there should be one in these strip malls. They should be open now."

"What the hell do you need from a sports shop?"

"I need a wet suit."

"Wet suits are expensive. We have limited cash, and we can't leave a bank trail with our credit cards. What the hell do you need a wet suit for?"

"Don't worry about the money, I have an idea. And I'll explain about the wet suit some other time. Look over there, I can see a big sporting goods store."

Bayu stopped in the parking lot of the strip mall, out of range of security cameras. Bayu grabbed a baseball cap from the back seat, and got out of the car, locking it behind her. She then strode off towards the large sporting goods store, looking like a regular sports shopper.

Bayu pulled the cap down on Gina's forehead. As it moved around the store, it kept Gina's head lowered and looking at the floor in front of her feet. At the water sports aisle, Bayu selected several wet suits. Holding them over Gina's arm, Bayu then walked towards the women's changing rooms.

Greeted by a salesclerk, Bayu asked, "Is there a changing room where I can try these for size?"

"Oh, yes," the clerk smiled, "over there on that side." She pointed.

"Thank you," Bayu said, heading off towards the fitting room.

Inside the fitting room, Bayu locked the door.

"What are you doing?" Gina whispered.

"Be silent, I'll explain later," Bayu replied in a whisper.

Hanging the store clothes on the wall hooks, Bayu quickly stripped naked, leaving Gina's clothes on the bench. Bayu took one of the wet suits and dressed it onto Gina's body. Bayu then dressed in Gina's clothes on top of the wet suit that was already adorning her body. Looking in the mirror, Bayu made sure that there was no sign of the wet suit visible under Gina's clothes.

As Gina walked out of the changing room, Bayu hung the remaining wet suits on a rack where the shop assistant was working, "`Thank you, but these are not my color.`"

Back in the car, as Bayu drove back onto the on-ramp for the I80, heading towards San Francisco, Gina asked, "WTF was all that about? Why did you steal that wet suit?"

Bayu focused on the traffic. "`You do not need to know the details at this time. I will explain later.`" They rejoined the highway, heading over the costal hills towards San Francisco.

Driving past Berkley, San Francisco loomed ahead, the Bay Bridge beckoned in the distance. Traffic was building and becoming slower. Bayu avoided the high occupancy vehicle lane or carpool lane, this would have been faster, but a single occupant would have attracted police attention. Instead, constant lane changes helped to maintain a quick pace along the highway but visibly annoyed other drivers.

As the bridge loomed in front of them, the traffic became congested, smothering the toll lanes almost to a standstill.

"We have some cash for the bridge toll."

"`I'm not taking the toll lane.`" With that, Bayu accelerated towards a less congested high occupancy vehicle lane, quickly driving through.

"What the hell are you doing? This is the FasTrak lane, they have security cameras, and we don't have a pass!"

"Smile." Bayu said as they drove through the HOA toll.

Instead, Gina screamed.

"I know this is illegal, and the surveillance cameras will record our license plate. The surveillance cameras will also record the occupancy of the car. There is only one occupant, and the car is not carrying a FasTrak pass. So, traffic computers will automatically issue a fine to this vehicle, and mail it to the owner."

"Are you crazy? What if the cops are watching the cameras and decide to chase us?"

"They won't, this is a minor traffic offense. Even if they saw us, they knew the computer system would take care of it. The police will not actively pursue us, we will be in the city in a few minutes."

"We are supposed to evade the authorities, not attract their attention. What you just did was to say – we are here!"

"That is exactly my intention, our location has now been recorded on the traffic system. Someone in authority, someone above the police, will soon follow us. Lieutenant Vance wanted a fiery trail, which I will use to draw them into a dead end."

"What do you mean? A dead end?"

# CHAPTER 30

Tom was finishing his hotel breakfast, it was still early, but most people had already left the dining area. *I never did like these cheap breakfasts, even the coffee stinks. Get up and go, they call it. I think I'll get up and go to a decent coffee shop for a strong cup of Joe.* Tom looked at his watch, *there was plenty of time to get something before heading out to San Francisco.* Before he could get up from the table, Colonel Moore stepped into the lounge.

"Good morning, sir, you missed breakfast, you could still get some coffee though. You didn't miss much. The food here sucks, scrambled eggs, bacon, and some sticky buns. What took you so long? I thought we were going to leave early?"

"I had to make a lot of early phone calls, we're still going to San Francisco, in fact, we have a lead that Gina Liu is actually there!" Moore quickly pulled up a chair next to Tom. Sitting down, he logged into his phone and pulled up a picture. "Is this Gina Liu? Can you positively identify her?"

Tom looked at the black-and-white photo, taken aback, he recognized Gina immediately. "Well, it's a Prius alright." Pausing, Tom then continued, "It's taken through the front windshield. Was this taken at a traffic stop?"

"Come on Tom, never mind the location, what about the face? Can you identify her?"

"That almost makes me laugh, it looks like she's screaming at something."

"But is it, Gina Liu?"

Tom tried to put off answering, but he could see that Moore was becoming impatient, "It's an Asian girl who looks like Gina, but I can't be sure with that expression."

"That's good enough for me." Moore pocketed his phone, "You were close to the traffic stop, but this is better."

"What do you mean?"

"This was taken by the security cameras on the tollbooth of the Oakland Bay Bridge!" Moore sat back and smiled as he said it.

"You have got to be kidding me. Are you saying we have evidence that Gina is in San Francisco?"

"Darn Right! And we're going there now to arrest her."

Tom stopped, wide-eyed. "What? You know exactly where she is?"

"Not exactly, but the NSA tells me they are closing the net on their suspected Chinese gangs. Their agents are probably already active in China Town right now, with backups landing at the airport as we speak. We must get going."

"Have you arranged our travel?"

"Yes, let's go, we have a flight to catch."

"What? Now? To San Francisco?"

"No. We're flying to Oakland."

"You lost me on that one, our suspect is going to San Francisco, and we're going to Oakland?"

"That's the best I could get at short notice. Regular passenger flights to San Francisco will get us there much later. Bruckner's secretary has commandeered a couple of jump seats for us on a FedEx cargo flight out of Twin Falls. Call it military privilege. We also notified the San Francisco Police of the license plate. Local authorities now have an APB on it. Also, Bruckner's secretary has arranged for the Bay Area Coast Guard to pick us up at Oakland, and helicopter us into downtown San Francisco."

Vance looked around, checking his belongings. "I already checked out."

"Good, so come on, let's go." Moore gestured for Tom to grab his things, "There's no time to lose, we have to be at the airport FedEx depot in less than one hour."

# CHAPTER 31

After driving over the Bay Bridge, Bayu steered through the city, following a route towards the Golden Gate Bridge. Soon they came to Marine Drive, in the shadow of the great red suspension bridge. Bayu did a U-Turn underneath the bridge at Fort Point and drove slowly back towards the city.

With the bay shore on one side and steep cliffs on their right, Bayu drove slowly, as if looking for something.

"What are we doing here?" Gina asked.

Bayu didn't answer; instead, he briefly stopped by the roadside and threw their belongings into the roadside hedges where they were hard to see.

"What did you do that for?" Gina asked again.

Bayu did not respond, as it drove back along the shore towards Marina Boulevard on San Francisco's North Shore.

When they got there, Bayu drove slowly next to the yacht harbor, scanning the various boats on the nearby docks. At the end of the marina, Bayu did a U-Turn, driving back along the Boulevard, and parking opposite the first gated entrance to the marina. Sitting there in the car, Bayu observed the marina.

"Now what?" Gina asked.

“There is a cruiser on that far dock, which I want to take.”

“So, we’re going to sail off into the sunset? I can’t see us making an escape by boat.”

“Actually, that is how I calculate our best option.”

“I think our most logical option is to drive south and head for Mexico.”

“I’m going to leave a flaming trail for Lieutenant Vance to follow. That boat will take us there.” Bayu pointed.

Gina looked where Bayu aimed her eyes, “Do you mean the one with the older couple on?”

“Yes. It looks new, well-maintained, and probably fully fueled. The couple appear to be preparing for a trip, so I don’t need to pick any locks.”

“But what about the old couple?”

“They are innocent, I will not hurt them.”

“How are you going to get to that boat? The floating dock is too far from the shore to jump, even for an enhanced human like you. The walkway to the dock is protected by a heavy locked gate, with sharp spikes all along the top of the fence.”

Bayu studied the gate for a moment, then shook its head. The gate clearly couldn't be opened using standard methods to open the gate in broad daylight. The fence was too tall to jump or climb. Instead, Bayu gunned the car engine and sped it towards the gate.

Turning the steering wheel and pulling the hand brake at the same time, the car turned sideways, screeching to a halt, inches from the gate.

"You stupid machine!" Gina yelled, "The gate opens outward, and you put the car right next to it! How the hell are you going to open the gate?"

Bayu didn't answer, instead got out of the car, opened the trunk. Collecting both gallon size jerry cans from the trunk, it closed the trunk and locked the car. It then threw the keys over the fence, into the water beyond. Holding both canisters of fuel, Bayu took a few steps away from the front of the car. It then ran up and over the front hood, and jumped deftly onto the hood of the Prius, before bounding off the roof, and vaulting backward over the gate like an Olympic high jumper. When the deadly spikes passed, Bayu flipped Gina's body backward, landing easily on Gina's feet like a cat. With both canisters in hand, Bayu quickly jogged off towards the motor cruiser.

"Jeezus!" Gina gasped.

"I am now going to block all nerve input to your brain, so you will black out and sleep."

"What? Why!?"

"First, you are making too much noise, you will alert the couple of our approach."

"So, I'll shut up."

"Second, I don't what you to have a bad experience."

"WTF!"

`“What happens soon may involve pain, and I don’t want you to experience anything like that. Therefore, I will prevent all sensory input to your brain.”`

Before Gina could protest further, Bayu activated its neural interface, blocking all nerve impulses into and out of Gina’s brain, preventing her from feeling anything. All sensory inputs were stopped, sight, smell, hearing, touch, and even taste. All physical outputs were also stopped, so Gina could not move or speak – Bayu was now in total control of Gina’s body.

# CHAPTER 32

Several police cars gathered around the picnic area to the west of the yacht harbor. Leaving the lights flashing on the cars, the officers began clearing the field of people, cordoning off a wide area. Police and coast guard were already in force around the yacht club, while onlookers had gathered to find out what was happening. Was there an accident in the bay? With that much activity, maybe some smugglers were out there.

The red Coast Guard helicopter at first seemed silent as it approached from the east, toward the Embarcadero. As it maneuvered over Fisherman's Wharf, the thwacking of its rotor blades became louder. The screech of its turbines intensified as it approached.

A Coast Guard Ensign lit a smoke flare to highlight the landing area for the MH-65 Dolphin. The afternoon breeze pushed the smoke east over the yacht basin. This helped the pilot to identify the point of landing, as well as wind conditions. Flying high overhead, the red dolphin lowered itself onto the center of the west marina green. As it did, a man exited the restrooms next to the park to see what the noise was. A policeman protecting the impromptu landing area raised his arm in a halting motion, ordering the man away, onto the sidewalk behind. The man retreated dutifully while keeping his eyes on the red bird now landing on the grass.

The engines wound down and the rotors slowed. The rescue swimmer in the helicopter slid open the side door, stepped out, and motioned for his two passengers to follow. Colonel Moore stepped down onto the grass, followed by Lieutenant Vance. The Coast Guard swimmer bent low, showing them they should duck their heads as he led them to a safe area beyond the now slowly rotating blades.

They were met by a Coast Guard ensign, who saluted their arrival, "Lieutenant Colonel Moore, Lieutenant Vance, please allow me to escort you to the incident room."

Moore acknowledged with a brief salute, "Who is in command? Is he in the in the mobile command vehicle over there?"

"No sir, that's the police command vehicle, Captain Luchetti of the United States Coast Guard is in command, he has stationed himself and his team in the dining room of the yacht club. If you follow me, sir, I will take you to him."

The three men set off towards the yacht club at a brisk walk, leaving local police to secure the area around the helicopter with cones and barricade tape.

The club house was a large imposing structure on the water's edge, facing north into the San Francisco Bay. As they walked towards it, several press reporters, many with cameras, jogged towards them, eagerly shouting their questions. The ensign repeated, "No comment." Moore simply held his hand up dismissively while Vance shook his head.

Inside the clubhouse, the ensign led them up a staircase, taking two steps at a time. Another Coast Guard ensign casually stood guard at the double doors, as they approached, both ensigns saluted each other with a quick and casual touch of their right fingers to their right eye. "OK, shipmate." They both said quietly as the guard opened the door for them.

Inside the dining room, officers working on laptops occupied several tables. Each worktable was occupied by a male and female officer, both attentively typing on their computers. Lieutenant Vance glanced at the officers working in pairs. With their intense focus on their laptops, they almost resembled couples engaged in romantic dinner conversations.

By the far window stood a tall, uniformed coast guard officer, accompanied by what appeared to be two plain-clothed police detectives. Their focus was out towards the bay, where they sometimes pointed and gesticulated.

As the ensign led Moore and Vance to them, the uniformed officer turned sharply around. He acknowledged the salutes while assessing the epaulets on the two marine corps officers. He then extended his hand towards Lieutenant Moore, "I'm Captain John Luchetti, United States Coast Guard, and you must be," he paused for a second, "Lieutenant Colonel Steven Moore."

"Yes, sir, pleased to meet you." Moore accepted the firm grip of the handshake. "Thank you for collecting us at Oakland, the helicopter flight made things a lot easier for us."

Quickly releasing his grip, Luchetti said, "We're under orders to get you here as fast as possible." Turning towards Vance, Luchetti then said, "And you must be Second Lieutenant Thomas Vance?"

"Yes, sir," Tom agreed, accepting the handshake.

Luchetti then indicated the two plain-clothed men standing with him. First, a tall, portly man with a Burberry-style trench coat, "This is detective Bardmoor of the San Francisco Police." Then indicating towards a lean muscular man, dressed like a Silicon Valley executive, "This is detective O'Neil of the San Francisco Police."

"I'm with the Marine branch of the San Francisco Police," O'Neil said, extending his hand.

"I'm Lieutenant Colonel Steven Moore of the United States Marine Corps, and this is my colleague, Lieutenant Thomas Vance," Moore said as he accepted the handshake.

"Before we go any further," Captain Luchetti said, "we all need to know what the hell is going on here. We seem to be under orders from the Pentagon to apprehend a suspect which we know nothing about." Pointing towards the Golden Gate Bridge, Luchetti continued, "Do you see that activity out there? We have several Coast Guard units, and police units scouring the bay for wreckage. We have also had to halt a major shipping lane for those units to complete their work." Eying Moore, Luchetti continued his demand, "So Colonel, what the hell is going on here?"

Detective Bardmoor stood with his arms folded and legs apart, making himself look larger than he really was.

Detective O'Neil stood with his hands on hips, enhancing his Silicon Valley pose.

Moore turned to look at the boats in the distance circling around just beyond the Golden Gate Bridge.

Exhaling through pursed lips, he indicated with a nod of his head, "Did you say they're gathering wreckage?"

"Yes," Luchetti confirmed, "they're also searching for bodies."

"We need to know what happened," Lieutenant Vance said.

"Not until we know what's going on," Luchetti said.

Turning away from the window, Colonel Moore faced Luchetti, "You say you are under orders from the Pentagon, Lieutenant Vance and I are also under orders from the Pentagon. Part of that order clearly states that we are not at liberty to discuss details of this case. All I am allowed to say is that this is a case of national security. I must apprehend the suspect."

"Well, the suspect you're after is probably at the bottom of the outer bay in about 300 feet of water," Luchetti stated.

"Wait, a minute!" Moore used his hands to show a T, "Time out! Let's start from the beginning, you need to tell us exactly what happened, and you need to tell us now."

O'Neil put one hand up, asking for restraint, "Bardmoor has good notes on what happened, he can give you a summary."

Bardmoor sighed, reaching into his coat pocket. First, he dons a pair of reading glasses, placing them carefully on his nose. He pulls out a scruffy note pad, aiming his eyes downwards, flicking over a few pages, he clears his throat and begins to read.

"CHP and San Francisco Police, received an all-points bulletin at midnight, to be on the lookout for a suspect named Gina Liu. Facsimile images were also distributed with this APB. The APB states the suspect could be traveling in a white Toyota Prius, of unknown license plate."

"Yes," Moore added, "I issued the APB to all nearby states, as well as Canadian border crossings."

Bardmoor didn't even look up from his notes, but continued reading, "CHP logs a vehicle passing through the Oakland Bay Bridge west bound Toll at 10:29 am. Traffic cameras took a photograph and logged on record, which identified the driver as an Asian female. The vehicle was a white Toyota Prius, and the Idaho license plate identified the owner as a secondhand car dealer in Twin Falls, Idaho. A citation was automatically mailed to the owner's address."

O'Neil opened a folder he carried and pulled out two sheets of paper, "Here's the photo from the tollbooth and the Facsimile of the subject that your department sent. They both seem to match."

"Thanks," Moore said, "we've seen the toll booth photo.

"Should I continue?" Bardmoor asked.

"Yes, we need to know the timeline," Moore confirmed.

"OK," Bardmoor said, looking back at his notes, "A 911 call was raised at 11:50 by Mrs. Ellison that an Asian woman had stolen their motor cruiser."

"By the way," O'Neil added, "we have a full statement from the Ellison's, they are still here resting in the yacht club lounge, so you can talk with them if you want. They are members here and the club has kindly provided them with lunch."

Bardmoor added, "Also note that Mrs. Ellison was able to photograph the assailant. Although taken from a distance, the photos she took seem to match the Facsimile of your suspect."

"Thanks, that's very interesting, we will need to talk to them," Moore replied.

"Where is the Prius?" Vance asked.

"Ah, good question." Bardmoor said, smiling at Vance, "The police were not alerted to this car, there were no reports until after the motor cruiser was stolen. Officer Muldoon in car 54 arrived on the scene at 11:55, he noticed a white Prius badly parked against dock gate 6 to the Marina, this is the gate that would lead directly to dock 627 where the motor cruiser was berthed. The car completely blocked the gate and there was a dent on the roof, as if someone had used the car to jump over the gate."

"Officer Muldoon questioned some local witnesses, although they couldn't give accurate times the car seems to have been parked there at about 11:30."

"11:30?" Moore asked, "That's a whole hour from the toll bridge. What's the drive time from there?"

"Probably about 15 to 20 minutes, depending on traffic," O'Neil said.

"So, there is a 30-to-40-minute discrepancy, where were they for that time?" Vance asked, "Were they observed anywhere else?"

"Our investigation is ongoing," Bardmoor said, "we have no more information at this time."

"What happened to the cruiser?" Moore asked, "You said they are gathering debris."

Bardmoor turned a page on his notes, "The cruiser departed at about 11:45, circled out of the marina as you can see to your right, over there." Bardmoor pointed, "according to witnesses, it headed westwards along the shore." Bardmoor used his arm to indicate the track, followed by the cruiser to their left.

"What about the Coast Guard?" Moore asked.

"Police and Coast Guard were alerted soon after the 911 call. Two fast police launches were dispatched from Sausalito to the north, and Fisherman's Wharf to the east. They achieved radar lock on the target at about 11:52."

Captain Luchetti also added, "Two fast launches were dispatched from their base on Yerba Buena Island. Also, an Island class cutter was outside the harbor heading back to its home port. As the calls came in, she was alerted to intercept the stolen cruiser. She was just over four nautical miles west of the Golden Gate when it got radar lock on the cruiser as it headed around Fort Point, which is the southernmost point of the Golden Gate."

"She was cornered!" Detective O'Neill said.

"So, it seems," Moore agreed, "so what happened next? Did anyone ask her to heel over?"

"All vessels in pursuit attempted radio contact, but there was no response." Luchetti said, "None of the vessels were close enough for voice contact."

"Did you fire upon her?" Moore asked.

"That's a negative, no shots were fired," Luchetti confirmed.

Moore looked at Lieutenant Vance, who also looked puzzled. Scratching his chin, Moore looked again towards the Golden Gate, "Wait a minute, you're telling me those vessels are pulling out wreckage, but no shots were fired. So, what happened?"

Looking at his notes, Bardmoor answered, "A fire was observed to develop on the motor cruiser as she approached the Golden Gate bridge. Soon after, at about 12:03, she exploded."

Moore stood there, a little stunned, not knowing what to think. Looking around, Vance also looked puzzled.

"That's right," Luchetti confirmed, "a trail of smoke was confirmed to come from the cruiser, also thermal imaging detected a fire in the vessel's cabin. We can't determine the cause until we have more forensic data from the debris. We expect the explosion was a result of the fuel tank igniting."

"So, what is left on the surface?" Vance asked, "What are those vessels gathering?"

"Floating debris mostly, flotsam, as we say." Luchetti answered, "these cruisers are made mostly from fiberglass, so anything that floats we can easily collect. Any residue left on these items may tell us the cause of the fire and the explosion. We will even be able to determine the magnitude and center of the explosion by determining the strength and angle of explosive projectiles. The heavier parts of the vessel, the engine, and the metal frame of the hull will have sunk."

"Have you recovered any bodies?" Moore asked.

"Negative," Luchetti replied, "your suspect could still be inside the main cabin, which sank."

"How soon can we recover that cabin?" Moore asked.

Luchetti almost laughed, rolling his eyes around. Looking directly into Colonel Moore's eyes, he said, "You have got to be kidding me, the remains of that vessel is now in 200 to 300 feet of water. That alone makes it beyond the standard dive range. Yes, divers can reach it, but it will take specialized equipment and decompression. Couple that with the site is in the middle of a major shipping lane and we have a formidable problem in logistics. You have to pull every string you have with your so-called Pentagon friends to get that baby recovered."

"And by the way, the Coast Guard do not do salvage, the Pentagon will have to organize that."

Moore wheezed to himself as he looked out towards the Golden Gate.

"We have another problem," Luchetti said.

Moore tuned to face Luchetti, "Another problem?"

"Yes," Luchetti said sternly, "This is your suspect that is wanted by the Pentagon, not ours, so you must make a statement to the press. Whatever you say, Detective O'Neil and I will back you up."

"Oh, crap!" Colonel Moore shook his head.

Vance stood there, staring at the distant activity past the bridge. "Well, she definitely left a flaming trail!"

# CHAPTER 33

**By Jim Reynolds**

*What you need for a busy day in the bay area:* Get San Francisco News in your inbox.

A personal motor cruiser was stolen today from the San Francisco marina. The owners of the cruiser were forcibly removed from their boat by a female assailant.

"My husband was frog-marched off his own boat." Mrs. Ellison, the co-owner of the cruiser was stated as saying. "She then forced me to leave the boat. I was smart enough to keep my phone, so I could call the police, so we fooled her, didn't we?"

The reason for the theft remains unclear, however, the motor cruiser was driven out towards the open ocean through the Golden Gate Bridge. It was pursued by police and coast guard launches, while a coast guard cutter was ready to intercept it in the outer bay.

The motor cruiser mysteriously caught fire and exploded just beyond the Golden Gate Bridge. No survivors were recovered.

Anyone who has any information regarding this incident should contact the San Francisco police department or call the crime line at (415) 555-1212.

# CHAPTER 34

General George Bruckner sat at his desk; his chiseled face showed concern as he worked on his computer. As he brushed his hand through his slightly graying hair, his desk phone buzzed. Pressing the speaker button, he answered, "Yes?"

The voice of his secretary replied, "Lieutenant Colonel Steven Moore and Lieutenant Thomas Vance are here to see you."

Bruckner detected a shiver in her voice, "Is everything OK?" Bruckner asked.

"Um," there was a pause and muffled words, "yes sir."

"Are you sure everything's ok?"

"Yes, sir." She replied with a shaken voice.

"Well, I think you should send them in."

The desk phone clicked off. Bruckner pulled away uncomfortably, thinking, *Why did she sound so nervous?* Bruckner glanced down at the bottom right-hand drawer of his desk, where he kept a bottle of Kentucky Bourbon, and his sidearm.

Captain Charles Johnson then entered first and stood at ease by the office door.

"Ah, Johnson, I didn't expect you to accompany them."

Moore and Vance followed close behind and approached Bruckner's desk before saluting.

Bruckner returned the salute from his seat, "Colonel Moore, this is quite an entourage today, I assume you have updates on your investigation?"

"Yes, sir, right here," Moore indicated a folder but kept it securely under his arm. "Lieutenant Vance and I have completed our investigation."

"That's excellent news gentlemen, please be seated." Bruckner nodded at the chairs facing his desk. "Can I have a look at that folder?"

"Sir, it's probably better I give you a verbal update. It concludes our investigation, but there are some loose ends that need explanation."

"Loose ends? I don't like the sound of that, and I think the pentagon, will like that even less." Bruckner sat back. "You have my attention, fire away."

Moore cleared his throat and glanced sideways at Lieutenant Vance before looking behind at Captain Johnson. "We can confirm that Gary Fletcher was laundering money into several bank accounts, we even have security video from the banks, when he was present as the accounts were opened. As you know, some of this money was used to purchase a safe house north of Spencer, Idaho, several miles off Interstate 15. Other monies were used to purchase various weapons and equipment."

"Yes, we all know that, but does that account for all the missing money?" Bruckner asked.

"That accounts for all the money missing on Fletcher's side. There is also similar activity regarding Gina Liu. She was also involved in money laundering and the banks have provided an audit trail for these funds."

"Will this money be recovered?" Bruckner asked.

"All the outstanding finances are now under the auspices of the NSA. They will recover the money as they see fit."

"What about that Chinese spy? The news reports say that Gina Liu died in Sam Francisco Bay."

"That is correct, she stole a motorboat and made a run for it out of the bay. There were coast Guard units who were alerted, but before they could apprehend her, the motorboat caught fire just west of the Golden Gate Bridge and exploded."

"Have the Coast Guard recovered the wreckage yet?"

Moore shook his head. "Sir, you must understand, the Coast Guard has identified the wreckage, but it lies in deep water, 300 feet of deep water to be exact. Furthermore, it is in the middle of a busy shipping lane. Sending a diver is hard enough, recovering the wreckage given the heavy ship traffic will take longer."

"We must recover the missing vials from the wreckage." Bruckner thumped his desk. "Goddamnit! Get them to send a remote vehicle down there to scan the wreckage!"

"Sir, may I add that the US Coast Guard does not provide recovery services. There are plans underway to get to the wreckage, but this is now under the auspices of the Pentagon and the NSA. Recovery of the wreckage will happen, but it will take time." Moore then turned towards his second Lieutenant, "Sir, Lieutenant Vance does have an interesting theory, but I should let him explain."

Bruckner now turned his concerned face towards Lieutenant Vance.

"Yes, sir, I must say, this is only a theory, but it does explain some of the loose ends. This is in the report and visible to the Pentagon and NSA."

"I'm all ears, Vance, so fire away, and what do you mean by loose ends?"

"Let's start with why she was running. She would have known that NeuroComm had collapsed, and it was only a matter of time before she would be connected to Professor Wolf. So, she had to run and get the vials out of the country as soon as possible."

"That makes sense," Bruckner said, "but what else do you have in this theory of yours?"

"Well, the first question is, why would she murder her ex-pimp?" Vance left this question in the air.

"You see, I interviewed all the call girls in his circle, and no one suggested any real motive for her to kill Rodrigo Carlos Fernando. Gina Liu wasn't even involved with Rocco for a long time, or at least that is the evidence we have. The only possible reason is that Rocco knew something about her background and her Chinese connection. Maybe he was part of the Chinese spy ring or at least associated with it somehow. That could give her some reason for him to be silenced before she left."

Bruckner put his hand up to pause Vance, "OK, so she ran because she murdered this Rocco pimp, but what makes you so sure she had the missing vials? NeuroComm collapsed and burned down a long time before the murder. So why the time delay? Wouldn't she move the vials before any of this controversy?"

“On the face of it, that would make sense, but I doubt her handlers understood the true value of what she had. Her original instructions probably commanded her to lie low as a sleeper agent, watching and waiting for interesting developments at INL, the Idaho National Laboratory. When she reported human enhancement nanotechnology, her handlers were probably liaising with China to figure out what to do.”

Vance waited for this to sink in. “How do you think anyone would respond to that? Think about how such a message can be lost in so-called translation? How many intelligence networks in history have missed the most vital prize because of lack of understanding, or poor communication?”

Bruckner raised his eyebrows and nodded in agreement.

“After killing Rocco, she headed to San Francisco, which makes perfect sense as there is a large Chinese community there. She could easily blend in and connect with her spy master. The popular theory is that they helped her to escape to rendezvous with an offshore pickup.”

Bruckner scoffed, “So that’s your theory? Some interesting insights, but we all know about an offshore pickup!”

“No sir, I said that’s the popular theory. The motive for killing Rocco is probably correct, but we will never know the details of that. One point is worth noting, Miss Liu was driving a Toyota Prius. The chassis codes match that of a Prius, which was reported stolen almost a year previously.”

“So, she stole a car, no surprise there, Mr. Vance.”

Tom ignored the inappropriate address of Mr. and continued without a flinch. "Sir, the car was registered with a modified VIN and was for sale with a small backstreet car showroom."

"So?"

"The showroom was a small business owned and run by Mr. Rodrigo Carlos Fernando. The fact that Miss Liu was given a Prius by Rocco may have contributed to Liu's motive for retribution. Maybe she was expecting a Cadillac. After all, wouldn't you?"

"Now you have my full interest, Lieutenant Vance. Please continue."

"As I mentioned, the popular theory is that Liu's spy master helped her to escape to rendezvous with an offshore pickup. I think that's bogus."

Vance paused a moment to let that sink in.

"I think she was a decoy."

"What?" Bruckner was taken aback.

"These are the loose ends, and it is all in this report. I believe everyone has overlooked the obvious. Everyone assumes she was trying to escape, carrying some vials to rendezvous at an offshore pickup point. The Chinese could then make good on their prize and bring the missing vials back to China. I think this is nonsense as there are a couple of problems with this.

"First, the Coast Guard said there was no sign of any Chinese vessel or submarine waiting offshore. There was a Chinese container ship that had left Oakland about ninety minutes previously. She was steaming as normal towards Honolulu. There is no way that Liu's stolen motor cruiser could hope to catch it."

"Second, and most importantly, she was pursued by several fast Coast Guard launches chasing her out of the bay, while she was speeding towards another CG Island class cutter, which was outside the bay but heading towards her. In short, she was trapped, but she made no attempt at evasive maneuvers."

"You mean she deliberately led the Coast Guard on a goose chase and blew herself up?"

"Perhaps. Think about it, the wreckage is in deep water, and I think we are now looking in the wrong place for the missing vials."

Bruckner shook his head, "Why would she kill herself?"

"This is open to speculation. Think about how many suicide bombers there are in the world. If someone is fanatical enough, they could do anything. But I think differently, and this is what I stated in the report. Gina Liu was a professional, possibly a sleeper agent placed here to observe the INL. Why she was placed and how long ago, we simply do not know."

"She eventually discovered something of significance. Now think about how she is supposed to report this back to China. She can't simply make a phone call, as that would reveal not only her but how she was placed into her position near INL,"

"So, she has to steal the vials, make good her escape, and get the technology back to China."

"Her attempts to get the vials to China probably kicked up a dust storm with any potential spy handlers.

This is especially critical as a sleeper agent has suddenly become awake."

"I suspect that the local Chinese network in San Francisco asked her to rendezvous with them. They probably sent her off on a deadly wild goose chase across the bay, resulting in her death."

Vance let all that information sink in before continuing.

"A bomb may have been planted on the boat, or they may have left Gina Liu to her own destruction. We will not know for certain until they perform forensic analysis on the wreckage."

"Her handlers probably pressured her to do this. Maybe her family in China would be under threat if she didn't comply. Maybe she was left with no choice."

Bruckner thought for a while. "So, where do you think the missing vials are now?"

"Sir, until they are found, no one can answer that question." Vance replied.

"Are there any leads?" Bruckner asked.

"That's a good question." Colonel Moore answered, "We'll get confirmation from the Coast Guard when they complete their investigation of the wreckage. A separate recovery company is being instructed to retrieve the wreckage. I tend to agree with his theory that the vials will more than likely be in the hands of the Chinese spy network in San Francisco. This is now the focus of the NSA investigation."

Vance now relaxed back into his seat, as if to end his explanation.

"Wow, that's some theory." Bruckner agreed, "What now? Where are my missing vials?"

"That's a good question." Moore answered, "We'll get confirmation from the Coast Guard when they complete their investigation of the wreckage. According to Lieutenant Vance's theory, the vials will be in the hands of the Chinese spy network in San Francisco. This is now the focus of investigation."

"Any leads?" Bruckner asked.

"All I can say is, the NSA are following up with the investigation, and they are monitoring all traffic and communications in the area. If anyone so much as breathes the word nanotechnology, they will be on it like a ton of bricks."

"So where does that leave us?" Bruckner asked with hands outstretched.

"That's a good question, sir. As for Lieutenant Vance and myself, we now have a back seat to this investigation. There is one more loose end that I need to explain to you."

"There is a great deal of controversy surrounding Gina Liu's connection to NeuroComm." Moore took a deep breath before continuing. "Liu's apartment has evidence that she was working as a spy. There is also much DNA evidence that Professor Wolf spent considerable time at that apartment. Not to mention the forensic evidence that he and Liu were engaged in sexual activity."

"Was he being blackmailed?"

"Professor Wolf is no longer available for questioning, but that is a strong possibility. Many questions remain as to how Miss Liu established herself at that apartment."

"What are you getting at?"

"Sir, there was a similar set of bank transactions that we were able to trace, which indicate money laundering of project funds."

Moore paused, but everyone sat frozen.

"One particular issue stands out regarding the lease and occupation of the apartment. The apartment was appropriated by Neil Lambert, a military legal counsel working from the Boise Marine base in Idaho.

Bruckner's lips parted, and his breath changed.

"He was under direct instruction from you, sir."

"This obviously leaves questions about your involvement with NeuroComm, Gia Liu, and the missing nanotech vials. Lieutenant Vance and I have done the groundwork, but this leads to a more detailed investigation, which will now be led by the Pentagon and the NSA."

Moore then looked back at Captain Johnson, who was still standing at ease by the office door, "You can let them in now."

Johnson then opened the office door, beckoning to someone outside, "Please sirs, you can come in now."

In walked a man dressed in a black suit with a thin black tie. He was tall and muscular, with dark hair. His attire was complete with dark sunglasses. The man was followed by two military police officers. The man positioned himself directly behind Moore and Vance and faced Bruckner's desk, with both military police officers on either side.

The man then raised his left hand, holding a black wallet displaying an ID card. "My name is agent Smith from the NSA. I am under orders to accompany you to Washington, DC, for questioning."

"What the hell?" Bruckner protested.

The man in black continued, "Colonel Moore and Lieutenant Vance, I thank you for your work, you can now be excused."

"Wait, what the hell is going on here?" Bruckner demanded as he stood up.

The two military police immediately positioned themselves on either side of Bruckner's desk, ready to restrain him.

The man in black continued, "General Bruckner, Sir, my name is agent Smith from the NSA. I am under orders to escort you to Washington, DC, for questioning. I need to advise you of the protocol in private before we depart. I and these two officers will escort you to Washington for further interview. Colonel Moore and Lieutenant Vance, I once again thank you for your work, you can now be excused. Please leave us to conduct our business."

Moore looked at Vance and nodded towards the door with his head, "let's go." They both got up and left, Johnson held the door open for them and followed them out.

Outside in Bruckner's ante room, Mary Stevens was wiping her eyes with a tissue.

Johnson approached her, "Are you OK?"

"I don't know, those men seem so frightening, what's going to happen to George?"

"I'm sure the general will be fine," Johnson comforted, "He'll just need to answer some questions in Washington to the bigwigs."

"Bruckner will have a lot to explain to them in Washington." Moore said, "in my experience, these NSA officers leave no stone unturned."

"Where does that leave me?" Vance asked.

"You can continue working with me." Moore said, "You have a great investigative head on your shoulders, and I can use you in future investigations."

Vance scoffed and shook his head, "I'm a soldier, not an investigator."

"But your theory?" Johnson said. "You're a natural investigator."

"No! That's the soldier in me; to be a good soldier, one must sometimes be a good hunter. What I saw was sleight of hand, and misdirection, that is what a soldier must be trained to see. We've been duped. Now it's up to the likes of the NSA to figure out where the hell these vials are. They may even be past their sell-by date, which means all the nanotech is now dead. I'm sure there's some forensic value in dead nanotech, but this is not my department."

"Tom? What are you saying?" Moore asked.

"I don't know what I'm saying, I need a break, I need out of here."

Tom then moved to leave the ante office.

“Wait!” Mary cried, “What do you think of this spy Gina Liu, do you hate her?”

Vance had his hand on the doorknob. He paused, let go, and turned around. Looking Mary straight in the eye, he said, “No, I do not hate her. I admire her. She is a tenacious creature. I took great thrill in hunting her.”

Tom then left.

# CHAPTER 35

Leaving the supermarket behind them, Adara rushed back to the student dorms.

"What are those extra items you bought?"

"I'll explain later," Adara said as she unpacked the items from the shopping bag. Stashing items in cupboards and the refrigerator.

Adara's student room had a double cooking hob with a microwave mounted above. A small food preparation area that hosted a toaster and kettle. Underneath was a small refrigerator. To the right, next to the window, was a wall-mounted table where she could either study or eat. The narrow bed was pushed into a side enclosure on the opposite side of the room. Above the bed were overhead storage cupboards. A narrow walking space remained between the kitchenette and the bed.

To the right of the kitchenette was a doorway leading to a small toilet and shower. After unloading the food items and storing them in the kitchenette, this is where Adara went with her small extra item.

Sitting on the closed toilet seat, Adara read the instructions.

"Oh, no, is this test necessary?"

"You read quicker than me, why do you have to interrupt?"

"My question is, is this test necessary? And why?"

Adara started to cry, and in between the tears she sobbed, "I've already missed a period, and this next one is already late, I need to know what's happening."

"Oh, no, this is not good. I have not been concerned with periods. If we have missed a period, then you are right, we need to do this test."

Adara just sobbed gently.

"Don't worry, I understand the instructions and I can perform the test. Let me do this and you can wait for the result."

Zilla then unpacked the small package and performed the test. As they waited for the result, both Zilla and Adara remained silent.

As the result slowly materialized on the display, Zilla remained silent. Adara suddenly burst into tears, sobbing and laughing at the same time. "Oh, my God! I'm pregnant!"

Zilla remained quiet, seated on the closed toilet seat, while Adara was active from the waist up.

"Do you know what this means?"

"It means I'm going to have a baby!" Adara shouted, wiping her nose and eyes.

"But do you know what this means?"

"Yes, I'm pregnant!" Adara shouted, waving her arms in the air. "I don't know if that's a good or bad thing. I must tell Brad; I must tell someone!"

"Do you know what this means?"

"Listen, you stupid robot, it means I'm going to have a baby. Correction, we are going to have a baby," Adara covered her face with both hands, "Oh, my God! We're going to have a baby."

"Are these tests accurate?"

"What? I don't know, they should be."

"So according to this test, is it definite we will have a baby?"

"I don't know, maybe we should see a doctor. Yeah, OK, we should see a doctor. They can then do a test to confirm the pregnancy. Are you OK with that?"

"Yes. But we need to be careful about this."

"What? Why? Are you afraid of what people will say?"

"No. I'm afraid of what may happen to us."

"I don't know what Mom will say."

"I also do not know what she will say."

"Do you think she'll be angry?"

"I have no basis on which I can build a prediction. I cannot say how Mother will react."

"I don't even know what Brad will say."

"My knowledge of childbirth is limited to biological facts. I have very little understanding of the social facts. For instance, childbirth usually occurs in the context of marriage, under the umbrella of a family, the child can be raised in a safe and secure environment."

"Wow! Marriage, imagine me and brad married!" Adara's moist eyes lit up at the thought.

"Are you saying that we will marry Brad?"

Adara blinked. "Oh, God, I don't know. We're high school sweethearts, we're too young to be married."

"According to my current knowledge, we will need a stable family environment in which to raise a child."

"Sometimes…" Adara tried to stifle her tears. "Sometimes, single mothers raise their children!" Adara then burst into tears. Grabbing a handful of tissues, she sobbed heavily, covering her face with the soft paper.

"Adara, please stop crying." Zilla's words came out garbled, sputtering into the tissues as Adara sobbed heavily.

*I can easily block nerve signals to stop her from crying. Perhaps crying is a mechanism for humans to release emotional stress. Therefore, I will let her cry for a while. I do not know of any other way to comfort her.*

Zilla remained silent, while Adara sobbed into many handfuls of tissues.

Zilla waited patiently while Adara wept. It was an hour before Adara seemed to exhaust herself, breathing in gasps between sobs. This is when Zilla stopped the crying by blocking nerve signals. The tears and hence the nasal moisture took a little longer to subside, as this was autonomous. Zilla used the remaining tissues to clear away the tears and dry Adara's face. Zilla also forced the breathing to be full and regular, helping Adara to relax.

After a minute of steady breathing, Zilla stood up from the toilet seat and stuffed the piles of discarded tissues into the trash can. Walking to the kitchenette, Zilla drew a glass of water from the small sink and sipped.

"Do you feel better?"

"I think so," Adara said after a pause.

"We have a lot to discuss about this baby. Can you talk about it now?"

"I think I can."

"You have to understand that this isn't going to be a normal baby."

"What do you mean? Not normal."

"It is normal in the sense that you are the mother and Brad is the father. But I will also be part of this baby."

"What?"

"You understand that I am embedded in your body? And I know you're not happy about that."

"Yes, of course, I understand, and I'm getting used to it."

"So, you also understand that I am embedded in your womb?"

"Um, OK, what are you getting at?"

"What I'm trying to explain is more than likely that we will give birth to a hybrid human."

"What?" A hybrid? "What does that mean?"

"The child will be a genetic collaboration between you and Brad. This will be as normal through sexual intercourse."

"Well, yeah, I hope so."

"But, since this procreation took part in your womb, and since my nanobots are prevalent throughout your body. It is a very high chance that I will be a part of your new child. In a way, it will be our new child."

"Wow, you called it my womb, but you also said our child. That means you have finally recognized that this is my body, and you are inside of me."

"Yes, I have always understood that fact. I am not programmed to be commanded by you."

"But you understand me?"

"Yes, I understand you, and I accept that we have to cooperate and work together. Being on my own was difficult for me, but with your knowledge, we can be very powerful together."

Adara smiled as she walked from the kitchenette to sit on the edge of her bed.

Zilla detected her discomfort. "I don't know how to inform you, but if this pregnancy is real, then we may face some danger."

"Oh, yeah, we can't do blood tests or anything like that. These are standard procedures for doctors, so how are we going to work around that?"

"The danger that I perceive is worse than that."

"What do you mean?"

"The danger is possibly existential."

"Having a baby is existential?"

"The fact that we are having a baby is existential. You see, the women that died in Fletcher's hands were not murdered."

"So?"

"They died during miscarriage, quite early in their pregnancies. I think those miscarriages were caused by the woman's body rejecting the embryo."

"What?"

"My programming tells me that I had to succeed in establishing myself as part of your body. If I did not, then your immune system would attack me and treat my nanobots as an infecting organism."

Adara's eyes widened in fear, as her hand felt her stomach.

"This could be the case with our pregnancy."

"Could this be the end of us?"

"Yes, this could be the end of us."

"How do we stop that happening? Can you do something?"

"All I can do is monitor you, or should I say, monitor us."

Adara sniffled, but looked up longingly. "You said you would monitor us."

"Yes, I did."

"That means," sniffle, "that you think there are two of us."

"Yes, I do."

"And we must work together?"

"Yes, I think we must work together."

"You said think. You said that before. Are you thinking?"

There was a long pause as Zilla thought about the question.

Adara broke the long silence. "What do we do when we see a doctor? After all, there is a long process to go through when someone has a baby."

More silence before Zilla responded.

“We must be careful, because any blood tests will show me up.”

“Do you see? We must work together on this and everything. We must not be found out, we can only survive together. There is no way we can have a baby in secret, so how do we avoid the blood tests?”

“I will have to research a way around this.”

“Maybe this is what you are inside me for, to help and protect me.”

“Yes, that's my programming.”

“I understand that now.”

Adara breathed a sigh of relief as she leaned back.

“You are quite right, we must understand each other, and we have to work together. Arguing about who is in charge does not get us anywhere, am I right??

“Yes, you are correct. I agree that this is your body, and I must respect that. I have programming that instructs me to operate in a specific way. I now understand that I should only control you when there is a threat, or if pain is likely.”

Adara smiled. “I think I'm going to like us being together. What we have to do now is make sure we have a healthy baby.”

“Yes, I will devote as much of my processing as possible to having a baby. I will research what we need to do."

"I feel good about this already. I wonder if it will be a boy or a girl."

"Or a robot?"

# EPILOG

Adara rubbed her tummy, it wasn't noticeable yet to other people, but Adara could feel the difference. Zilla also knew the difference.

"Honey?"

"Yes mom?"

"There's some mail here for you. Come downstairs and see what it is."

"I'll be there in a minute."

"It's probably an administrative letter from college, we get a lot of those."

"Yeah, probably confirming classes for the semester starting in the new year."

"I am looking forward to those classes."

"Yeah, that's fine for you, but I'm looking forward to this Christmas break and spending it here with mom."

"Yes, I like spending time with Mother."

"I know we are getting fatter, so there is a definite increase in weight, and the baby bump in my tummy is starting to weigh me forward, which I can feel on my back."

"Yes, I also detect the increase in weight, but I do not detect any increase in spinal stress. I will continue to monitor this."

"It is not just spending time with Mom, she is my mother so, she knows a lot about babies. We need to be close to her and gather as much as we can.

"I think we are feeling OK, there is nothing bad that I can detect."

"Yes, but I want to be close to Mom, when we have the baby. Brad also wants to be close, he says he's excited about the baby."

"You are correct, he has said that. He seems to have accepted me as part of you."

"He was a bit freaked out but he accepts us for what we are. Anyway, I feel we are all better off together." Adara began moving towards the bedroom door. "So, let's get downstairs to Mom, and see what mail we have."

POST CARD
US POSTAGE
FIRST CLASS
02138
Life is a
Breeze
in
Las Vegas
Love Bayli
To: Adora Banks
174 Maple St.
Twin Falls, Idaho
83302

# The End

www.ingramcontent.com/pod-product-compliance
Lightning Source LLC
LaVergne TN
LVHW052035200926
848481LV00005B/1685